"Within the pages of this book you'll find thought-pr[o]
cause you to pause, reflect, and view yourself, life's [
different eyes. In a decade that has given us a cacop[
ods that even the most spiritually focused people ca[
time to stop acting like human *doings* and get back to what God created us to be:
human *beings*. Through *Unearthed*, explore a quieter and more introspective world
and your role in it. Working through this book alone or, as I recommend, through
small-group study will be a catalyst to deeper understanding of yourself, God, and
others in your life. Through the lens provided within these pages by Raj Pillai, discover how each one of us is individually and collectively a true masterpiece: a work
done with extraordinary skill, created and placed in the world by the one true God."

—*Dr. Bettie Ann Brigham, vice provost, Eastern University*

"To spend time with Raj Pillai is like a gift of a cup of hot chocolate on a cold winter
day, and this book is full of comforting encouragement from on high. Read it. Drink
deep. You'll have enough left to share with others."

—*Steve Sjogren, Kindness Outreach ministries*

"With a constant eye toward Scripture, Raj Pillai uses relevant examples and acces-
sible prose to help us learn more about the 'life that is life' and what it looks like to
live into our identities as God's masterpieces."

—*D. Michael Lindsay, president, Gordon College*

"Do you feel insignificant? Inadequate? Question your self-worth? Have you been
wounded by what others have said about you—by what you have said about yourself? Dig deep into *Unearthed*, and you'll discover the truth of how God sees you
and the masterpiece He created you to be. Highly recommended!"

—*Marlene Bagnull, author, conference director*

"Even as a pastor for nearly 30 years now, one of my greatest struggles is embracing the
way God made me and sees me. I know I am significant because of my position as a
child of God. My worth is not in my performance or what others think of me. Knowing
in your mind and believing in your heart are two different things. On a run this morning,
the demons of doubt began to get the best of me again. I then sat down and read Raj's
book. God's timing is always perfect. I received a jolt of energy and resolve like never
before to accept that I am a masterpiece from God on an amazing journey. If you read
this book, you will discover the very same thing."

—*Randy Frazee, senior minister, Oak Hills Church,*
author of Think, Act, Be like Jesus

UNEARTHED

DISCOVER LIFE AS GOD'S

Masterpiece

UNEARTHED

DISCOVER LIFE AS GOD'S
Masterpiece

RAJ PILLAI

NEW HOPE®
PUBLISHERS
Gospel-Centered. Missions-Driven.
Birmingham, Alabama

New Hope® Publishers
PO Box 12065
Birmingham, AL 35202-2065
NewHopePublishers.com
New Hope Publishers is a division of WMU®.

New Hope Publishers serves its authors as they express their views, which may not express the views of the publisher.

Library of Congress Cataloging-in-Publication Data

Names: Pillai, Raj, 1968- author.
Title: Unearthed : discover life as God's masterpiece / Raj Pillai.
Description: First [edition]. | Birmingham : New Hope Publishers, 2017.
Identifiers: LCCN 2017011590 | ISBN 9781625915221 (permabind)
Subjects: LCSH: Identity (Psychology)--Religious aspects--Christianity. |
 Self-perception--Religious aspects--Christianity. | Masterpiece, Artistic.
 | Creation (Literary, artistic, etc.)--Religious aspects--Christianity. |
 Christianity and art.
Classification: LCC BV4509.5 .P566 2017 | DDC 248.4--dc23
LC record available at https://lccn.loc.gov/2017011590

ISBN-13: 978-1-62591-522-1

N174120 • 0617 • 2M1

DEDICATION

She is a very special person who has made an enormous impact
on my four daughters, my family, and hundreds of children
around the world
through the hundreds of handicrafts she makes and sends to missions,
through the teaching of the Bible to the women in our church,
and through many countless acts of service.

She may think her life is ordinary and commonplace and routine,
but in reality she is one of the greatest examples
of God's millions of masterpieces I know.

Her name is Suellen Velthuis,
and she happens to be my mother-in-law.
This book is dedicated to her.

And to the millions of God's masterpieces who, like Suellen,
love selflessly, serve faithfully, and give joyfully.

We are, not metaphorically but in very truth, a Divine work of art, something that God is making, and therefore something with which He will not be satisfied until it has a certain character. . . . One can imagine a sentient picture, after being rubbed and scraped and recommenced for the tenth time, wishing that it were only a thumbnail sketch whose making was over in a minute. In the same way, it is natural for us to wish that God had designed for us a less glorious and less arduous destiny, but then we are wishing not for more love but for less.

— *C. S. Lewis*

CONTENTS

ACKNOWLEDGMENTS 17

INTRODUCTION 21

   You (Remixed) 25

PART ONE—THE HIDDEN MASTERPIECE 33

   Chapter 1—Hidden 35

   Chapter 2—Flea Market 39

PART TWO—FRAME 47

   Chapter 3—Everything/Nothing 49

   Chapter 4—Longing 55

   Chapter 5—Past—1 63

   Chapter 6—Past—2 71

   Chapter 7—Spark 81

PART THREE—PICTURE 87

   Chapter 8—Birth 89

   Chapter 9—God 95

   Chapter 10—Death to Life 105

   Chapter 11—New 115

   Chapter 12—Talents 125

   Chapter 13—One Cup 131

Chapter 14—Silence 139

Chapter 15—Remains 149

Chapter 16—Today 155

PART FOUR—GALLERY 165

Chapter 17—Mosaic 167

Chapter 18—Elysium 175

Chapter 19—Disruption 185

Chapter 20—Tension 193

Chapter 21—Unknowns 201

EPILOGUE 209

STUDY GUIDE 211

ADDITIONAL RESOURCES 221

ACKNOWLEDGMENTS

While writing a book can be a solitary effort, making a book is always a collaborative endeavor. I owe a deep debt of gratitude to a number of people who encouraged, supported, read, offered perspectives, edited, designed, and prayed with me in this journey.

It seems such an understatement to say I am indebted to my Lord for the finished work on the Cross, which enabled my new life in and through Him, which in turn led to the writing of this book for His glory and for His kingdom.

I am thankful to my wife, Erika, and our four daughters for the sacrifice of time over a period of six months as I diligently set aside several hours on my off days to write this book. Without their active and enthusiastic support, this book would not have been possible.

I am also grateful to the ministry of Mark and Huldah Buntain in Calcutta, India, where I first learned about Jesus, and to Eastern University in St. Davids, Pennsylvania, where I first, fully understood what it meant to pray, "Thy kingdom come, Thy will be done in earth, as it is in heaven."

I am indebted to the entire New Hope team:

To Mark Bethea, acquisitions and digital editor, who prayed with me before we finalized the book details, which set the tone for the entire process of working with New Hope

To editors Reagan Jackson, Sarah Doss, and Melissa Hall for the meticulous and fabulous editing work on the manuscript, including fact-checking quotes and statistics and factual information,

To Tina Atchenson, Meredith Dunn, and Maegan Roper
for the remarkable design and marketing of the book, and

To the New Hope doctrinal theologian, Joshua Hays,
for his insights into specific parts of the manuscript.

Last, but not least, I want to add a shout-out to my church—Damascus Road Community Church in Mount Airy, Maryland—where people bring people to meet Jesus, where hope is found, authentic love and acceptance are experienced, and the radical grace and joy of Jesus is dispensed with reckless abandon. You inspire me!

INTRODUCTION

Ephesians 2:10 tells us, "For we are God's master-piece. He has created us anew in Christ Jesus, so we can do the good things he planned for us long ago" (NLT).

Most Christians, at least internally, resist the idea that we were created to be God's masterpiece. What does that mean? How can we live as God's masterpiece in a world fraught with evil, sin, despair, conflict, and pain? Then we find out some of these issues are not just out there, they are inside of us as well.

Add to this our struggle to find meaning in the ordinary, peace in the busyness and the fullness of life, when life itself seems to be barely firing on one cylinder, and we end up in a tortuous process of trying to find God's will in the here and now. And wrestling with it often produces feelings of guilt, frustration, and dismay.

Starting with a story of how one man found a priceless document hidden behind an old painting and rickety frame at a flea market, we will discover how we trade God's best for us for a distorted view of who we really are. The real masterpiece we were created to be remains hidden behind other false paintings, trapped inside old frames.

When Jesus proposed the building of God's kingdom, not in a political arena but in the hearts of men, women, and children, it was a radical idea. Two thousand years later, the strategy hasn't changed. The idea is if we truly experience the zest for life that the Spirit of God can bring into our souls (abundant living that Jesus promised His followers), then the world will see a collection of millions of God's masterpieces, working in tandem, a tapestry of great, beautiful, and awe-inspiring design, bringing hope and healing to a hurting and needy world.

We struggle to find meaning in the ordinary,
peace in the busyness and the fullness of life,
when life itself seems to be barely firing on one cylinder.

YOU (REMIXED)

You have searched me, Lord, and you know me.

God knows you.

He can look deep inside of you.

Into your heart,

Into your soul,

Into your mind.

Like no one else,

Nothing is hidden from Him.

Not your past,

Not your present,

Not your future.

You know when I sit and when I rise.

God knows when you sit down and when you stand up.

He knows when you got up this morning,

He knows what you had for breakfast,

He knows what you did,

He knows where you work.

You perceive my thoughts from afar.

Anxious thoughts,

Hopeful thoughts,

Fearful thoughts,

Loving thoughts,

Scary thoughts,

Whiny thoughts,

Delightful thoughts.

You discern my going out and my lying down.

> God knows the route you take to work,
>
> He knows which radio stations are preset in your car,
>
> He knows which television shows you watch,
>
> He knows your preferred brand of shampoo,
>
> He knows your favorite grocery store,
>
> He knows what you order at Starbucks,
>
> He knows where you shop,
>
> He knows everything you do,
>
> He knows everywhere you go,

You are familiar with all my ways.

Before a word is on my tongue you, Lord, know it completely.

> Before you can speak, God knows which words you are
> going to use.
>
> Uplifting words,
>
> Biting words,
>
> Disheartening words,
>
> Joyful words,
>
> Cursing words,
>
> Comforting words,
>
> Judgmental words.

You hem me in behind and before,
and you lay your hand upon me.

> God is ahead of you and behind you at every moment.
>
> His presence is all around you.
>
> He is with you at work,
>
> At home,
>
> At school,
>
> At lunch,
>
> This hour,

This very moment,
His presence is all around you.
Such knowledge is too wonderful for me,
too lofty for me to attain.

Where can I go from your Spirit?
Where can I flee from your presence?
If I go up to the heavens, you are there;
if I make my bed in the depths, you are there.
If I rise on the wings of the dawn,
if I settle on the far side of the sea,

I can't hide from God.
If I climb Mount Everest, He is there.
If I go to the Dead Sea, He is there.
If I were to go beyond the galaxies,
Even there your hand will guide me,
your right hand will hold me fast.

If I say, "Surely the darkness will hide me
and the light become night around me,"
even the darkness will not be dark to you;
the night will shine like the day,
for darkness is as light to you.

God sees you in the dark.
In the darkest nights,
In the gloomiest, most depressing moments of your life,
He is there.

For you created my inmost being;

He knew when I should be born,
He knew where I should be born.

You knit me together in my mother's womb.

> God made me.
> He saw my unformed body,
> He knew exactly when I drew my first breath,
> My first heartbeat,
> My first strand of hair,
> My first grasp,
> My first cry,
> My first laugh,
> He knew. He saw. He made it possible.

I praise you because I am fearfully and wonderfully made;
your works are wonderful,
I know that full well.
I am fearfully and wonderfully made.

> The human body is a marvelous creation.
> Our heart will beat 35 million times a year.
> Our lungs will breathe in and out 1 million gallons of air
> each year.
> We have trillions of cells in our body.
> And our body produces millions of new ones each second.
> Our body is made of 640 muscles and 206 bones.
> An adult body has about 100,000 miles of blood vessels,
> which will carry millions of gallons of blood in our
> lifetime.
> Our eyes can detect 10 million different colors.
> The focusing muscles in our eyes move about 100,000
> times a day.
> We have 24,000 tiny hairs in our inner ears that act like
> strings of a piano and take information to our brains
> to decode sound ranges from a whisper to a locomotive.
> Our bones are as strong as granite.

We have 10,000 taste buds.

The human nose can distinguish between one trillion different smells.

The human body has a sophisticated immune system that can distinguish between pathogens and our own cells and lead an all-out vicious war against invading germs.

The brain has about 100 billion neurons and 100 trillion connections.

These connections can travel as fast as 250 miles per hour or more.

We can crawl, jump, run, walk, somersault, and bike.

I am fearfully and wonderfully made.

Your eyes saw my unformed body;
all the days ordained for me were written in your book
before one of them came to be.

Days when you don't feel very special.

Ordinary days, stressful days, dreary days.

Dark days, joyful days.

How precious to me are your thoughts, God!
How vast is the sum of them!
Were I to count them,
they would outnumber the grains of sand—
when I awake, I am still with you.

God's thoughts about you are vast and precious and immeasurable.

God actually thinks about you.

A lot.

He thinks of who He created you to be.

He thinks about the things He would like you to do.

He thinks of you being a light in the darkness.

He thinks about you living up to your soul's highest calling.
He thinks about you living a life of meaning, and significance, and purpose.
And He wants to shape you and mold you and lead you
on the path that is everlasting.

All this is true of me
and of you.

God wants to have a relationship with you, because
God made you.
God knows you.
God loves you.

You are a work of art.
One of a kind.

Masterpiece!

But do you believe it?
Can it be possible?
Is it visible, evident, and obvious?
Can everyone see it?
Or is it hidden, smeared, and shrouded?

—Based on Psalm 139

Part One
THE HIDDEN MASTERPIECE

We must be careful with our lives, for Christ's sake, because it would seem that they are the only lives we are going to have in this puzzling and perilous world, and so they are very precious and what we do with them matters enormously.

—Frederick Buechner, *Secrets in the Dark*

To be loved but not known is comforting but superficial. To be known and not loved is our greatest fear. But to be fully known and truly loved is, well, a lot like being loved by God. It is what we need more than anything. It liberates us from pretense, humbles us out of our self-righteousness, and fortifies us for any difficulty life can throw at us.

—Tim Keller, *The Meaning of Marriage*

Chapter 1

HIDDEN

ook back over your life. How much time have you spent analyzing, critiquing, and condemning yourself? Defining yourself by all the lousy things you have said and the awful things you have done? Have you ever labeled yourself a failure because of other people's thoughtless remarks, opinions, and judgments? Have you marked yourself inadequate, incompetent, and insignificant because of sin, regret, shame, and guilt and shut out God's whispers of healing, assurance, and love? Told yourself you are simply not up to the tasks, dreams, and longings you know God has planted in your heart?

If you have ever done this, you are not alone.

Throughout the Bible, God consistently, repeatedly, unwaveringly challenges people to be the best version of themselves that He created them to be in the first place.

But all too often, we find people in the Bible (and people in our time) start to believe in another version of themselves, they start believing someone else's version that covers up the real masterpiece.

God comes to Moses.

Moses raises a series of objections.

He feels inadequate.

He believes he lacks credibility.

He reminds God that he is not a great communicator.

God talks to Moses, tells Moses His dream, His plan, His purpose, and the role Moses is going to play in this epic story about to unfold, and Moses argues with God and in effect, says, "God, You don't seem to know me. You are making a big mistake. I can't do this!"

As a final plea, we find Moses saying to God, "Pardon your servant, Lord. Please send someone else" (Exodus 4:13).

Someone else? Moses, inside of you, there is a masterpiece waiting to come out.

King Solomon says to God, "Lᴏʀᴅ my God, you have made your servant king in place of my father David. But I am only a little child and do not know how to carry out my duties" (1 Kings 3:7).

Not a leader? Solomon, inside of you there is a masterpiece waiting to come out.

God comes to Jeremiah. God tells him how He formed him in his mother's womb and appointed him to be a prophet.

Jeremiah responds, "Alas, Sovereign Lᴏʀᴅ, I do not know how to speak; I am too young" (Jeremiah 1:6).

Too young? Can't speak? Jeremiah, inside of you, there is a masterpiece waiting to come out.

We think of the Apostle Paul as a hard-charging guy, but even he had his moments of fear and trembling (1 Corinthians 2:1–5).

Paul, inside of you, there is a masterpiece waiting to get out.

Which insecurities do you face when you think of becoming the masterpiece God made you to be?

I am too **YOUNG**.

I am TOO OLD.

I am too INADEQUATE.

I am *not brave* enough.

I CAN'T DO IT.

I am buried in **GUILT** and **SHAME**.

I am BROKEN, DAMAGED, WEAK.

People say I am a **LOSER**.

They say I am **NOT GOOD ENOUGH**,

SMART ENOUGH, **SPECIAL** ENOUGH.

My life is a MESS.

My story is a **DISASTER.**

My **FUTURE** is **IN DISARRAY.**

God made a MISTAKE when He made me.

The list is endless. But these are false pictures hiding the real masterpiece. All of these insecurities are like old, rickety frames.

Hidden behind these frames and false pictures is the real you. The new you God made when you came to Jesus. The best version of you.

The real you, the best you, is hidden. But it doesn't have to be. Let's embark on a journey to see what this masterpiece looks like.

Chapter 2

FLEA MARKET

everal years ago, we were vacationing in Pennsylvania when I stopped at a visitor center and picked up a *Pennsylvania Tourist* magazine. I read an article in it that caught my attention.

The article talked about this huge flea market in Adamstown, Pennsylvania. It's a collectors' paradise. Thousands show up every weekend. It is one of the largest flea markets of its kind.

In 1989, a man was walking around the Adamstown flea market when he saw an old picture. He didn't particularly like the picture itself, but he was drawn to the picture frame.

He asked the seller the price. It was $4.

He thought it was a bargain and immediately bought that old picture and frame for four bucks.

Later, when he tried to remove the picture, the frame, being very old, fell apart in his hands. But then he noticed something— lurking behind the picture was a folded document. He carefully unfolded the document and found it to be a copy of the Declaration of Independence—one of the original 500 copies first printed by John Dunlap in 1776 to take the news of the American independence to the 13 colonies. Only 23 copies were known to exist up until that time.

It was put up for sale by Sotheby's in an auction in 1991 and was sold for $2.4 million.

When I first read that story, I thought to myself that starting the very next year, and every year thereafter, we should probably be vacationing in Adamstown, Pennsylvania. All of a sudden, flea markets seemed like a good destination for a vacation!

Then I started thinking about the person who had placed the picture for sale. He had a masterpiece, but an old painting covered it up. And it was in an old frame that was falling apart. To him, his masterpiece was worth only $4. In other words, the person who owned the artwork before him had his masterpiece hidden to the point that the seller didn't even know he had one. He defined the value of what he owned by what was on the outside.

We too carry a junky looking picture. Each of us has one, bound with frames we are unable to break free from. We remain captive, hidden behind a painting that isn't us. Too much of our lives get invested in it, and change seems hard. We know we need to get rid of it, but we carry it around for way too long.

I know I hung on to my first car for far too long. It was a Ford Escort, and from the beginning, the car started giving me trouble. Within the first three years, the car went through two transmissions. That should have told me something. Fortunately, all of that was covered under warranty, but when the warranty ran out, the car continued to have problems. I started shelling out hundreds of dollars in repairs each year. Every time I spent money, I was hoping the car would last for another certain number of miles. Plus, I was determined for some unknown reason to make that car last 150,000 miles.

Well, after seven years, the car took a turn for the worse. First, there was the radiator and coolant leak, which cost me $800 to repair. Then the whole electrical circuit went out along with the air conditioner. That took another $1,000. Then the car blew something else here, broke something else there, and by June of that year, I had spent $2,800 in car repairs in three auto mechanic shops.

By this time, I was thinking, *I've spent so much money on this car, it has to last for 150,000 miles.* (I had 110,000 miles on it at the time.) Within a couple of weeks, a weird knocking sound started to come from the front of the car. I found out that a guy in my church was the best car doctor around—Doug. He very graciously offered to take a look. But I wanted an expert second opinion.

Doug drove the car, looked at it, and very kindly told me to get rid of the car. He said the prognosis was poor, and the car wouldn't last.

My father-in-law, in an attempt to cheer me up said, "You made some really dumb choices." No, he didn't say that. He told me he was sure the car was made on a Monday morning. He joked that all bad cars were made on Monday mornings.

A wise person would have taken Doug's advice, but not me. I was going to make that car last 150,000 miles at all costs. I could have gotten some money at trade-in for that car if I had listened to Doug. But I didn't.

Exactly two weeks later, the car suddenly broke into violent convulsions. It literally shook from side to side. Loud knocking sounds came from under the hood. Some of the lights on the dashboard were flashing, and a very ominous-smelling odor started pouring from the vents.

I managed to steer my car into a parking lot. There were people now looking at me. I barely pulled into the parking lot when there was a really loud bang. With one last gasp for life, the car stopped, and it felt like it sank a few inches.

I remember sitting there and thinking, "My car is dead." The next thought that struck me was, "Why on earth did I not listen to Doug?"

There was an auto mechanic's shop across from the parking lot. I ran over and got the mechanic to come look the car over. He said, "Yep, this baby's dead." He told me that coolant, oil, and gas were all leaking at the same time from under the car.

And then he looked at me and said, "What did you do to it?"

What did I do to it? I spent $2,800 trying to fix the thing!

And then he asked me if I wanted to take a look under the hood. I told him there wasn't going to be any last viewing. The funeral cost me another $150 (that's what he charged me to tow the car to the dump).

Why do we keep driving the Ford when we can see where it will lead?

And I don't mean the car.

We drive the Ford of sin, and it wrecks our lives. We know the way ahead leads only to meaninglessness and death, but we carry on. We feel like too much has already been invested. We can't seem to let it go. We think our circumstances cannot possibly change. We think we cannot possibly change.

We drive the Ford of bad decisions and rejection from our past. We drive the Ford of poor emotional and relational choices and can't seem to get ahead. We drive the Ford of shame and guilt.

It's time to get rid of the car. It represents all the things we keep investing in when we and others around us can see plainly that it is derailing our future, God's best, and us.

Perhaps we are afraid of the world seeing us the way God created us to be. We are afraid we might not live up to the promise of God. So we play small. We hide. We shrink. We downplay our God-given giftings and talents. We are afraid we are too insignificant to have a role to play in God's great kingdom drama.

We stop expecting God to do anything of great kingdom impact through our lives. We pray small prayers and exercise little faith. We start believing this is the best we can do. Worse, we start believing this is the best *God* can do.

And we sell ourselves short—we assign a value to ourselves that is far below what you and I are really worth.

Perhaps you have come to believe the old painting of you that is hiding the real you God made you to be.

The Bible declares we are God's masterpiece (Ephesians 2:10). But far too many of us have covered up the real masterpiece with a tattered old version of ourselves. Furthermore, many of us are trapped in an old frame (more on this in a moment).

Before we can be the masterpiece God created us to be, we need to allow God to dismantle the old, dusty, inferior, sin-stained, cheap, counterfeit picture of ourselves that we have placed upon our souls.

Let's go back to the flea market story. The seller had a masterpiece, but the masterpiece lay hidden behind another painting. And it was stuck inside an old, rickety frame.

It took someone to tear the old painting apart, to clear out the grime, the dust, the stain, and the filth. It took someone to break apart the old frames to reveal the real masterpiece—a Declaration of Independence.

In Paul's letter to the Christians in Ephesus, he writes,

> For we are God's masterpiece. He has created us anew in Christ Jesus, so we can do the good things he planned for us long ago.
>
> *—Ephesians 2:10 NLT*

We are God's masterpiece.

Jesus came to take away the grime, the dust, the stain, and the filth. He came to break apart the old frames that trap us and deceive us and bind us and chain us and enslave us, and on the Cross, He gave us the ultimate Declaration of Independence from sin, shame, and death.

**In Jesus, you have been healed,
you have been released, restored, redeemed, and reconciled,
you have been given this awesome new life in Christ.
To be a masterpiece.**

Yes, on the outside it may look like you are holding up OK; you are doing fine, you have control and have planned a life that is nice and comfortable and safe. But there is this gnawing sense, a question perhaps, that struggles to bubble up through life's distractions, demands, and difficulties, and it is this: with everything you have and own and enjoy, what is it that you really possess?

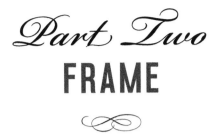

Part Two
FRAME

God has come to you to save the sinner. Be glad! This message is liberation through truth. You can hide nothing from God. The mask you wear before men will do you no good before Him. He wants to see you as you are, He wants to be gracious to you. You do not have to go on lying to yourself and your brothers, as if you were without sin; you can dare to be a sinner. Thank God for that, He loves the sinner but He hates sin.

—Dietrich Bonhoeffer, *Life Together*

Our job is not to deny the story, but to defy the ending.

—Dr. Brené Brown, *Rising Strong*

Chapter 3

EVERYTHING/NOTHING

*P*aul is writing a letter to the church at Corinth. In 2 Corinthians 6:4–5, he lists some of the things he had to go through because of his faith in Jesus:

Troubles

Hardships

Distresses

Beatings

Imprisonments

Riots

Hard Work

Sleepless Nights

Hunger

But then, Paul goes on to write some of the most astounding words, words that are fascinating, challenging, inspiring, and yet mysterious:

[We are] genuine, yet regarded as impostors; known, yet regarded as unknown; dying, and yet we live on; beaten, and yet not killed; sorrowful, yet always rejoicing; poor, yet making many rich; having nothing, and yet possessing everything.

—vv. 8–10

This passage made me wonder: Is the opposite possible? Is it possible to have everything, yet possess nothing? Is it possible to live under the illusion that we have everything but in reality have nothing?

In 2013, *TIME* magazine published a fascinating article titled "The Happiness of Pursuit." Author Jeffrey Kluger writes (about America):

Our long national expedition is entering its 238th year, and from the start, it was clear that this would be a bracing place to live. There would be plenty of food, plenty of land, plenty of minerals in the mountains and timber in the wilderness. You might have to work hard, but you'd have a grand time doing it.

That promise, for the most part, has been kept. . . . We created outrageous things just because we could–the Hoover Dam, the Golden Gate Bridge, the Empire State Building . . . We got to the moon 40 years later and . . . the tire tracks left on the lunar surface . . . are the real American graffiti.

This is an extraordinarily true commentary on our nation.

The article also lists how along the way, we invented many things—the light bulb, telegraph, movie camera, airplane, mass-produced car, polio vaccine, personal computer, smartphone, and social media to name a few.

Not only that, we spend unbelievable amounts of money for anything we want.

We are the richest, most well-resourced nation the world has ever known.

We have the best defense the world has ever known.

We have access to the best medical care the world has ever known.

We have the best freedom afforded to individuals, the common people, the world has ever known.

We have researched, studied, and microstudied every aspect of human existence and have more knowledge available to us at the click of a button than was available to any other group of human beings in all of human history.

So, then, here is something puzzling, intriguing, strange—if we are all that, how is it that, according to the same *TIME* article, only one-third of Americans say they are very happy? How is it that more than half of us, *TIME* reports, when we think of the future, are afraid of it?

How is it that according to research by the Mayo Clinic, other than antibiotics, the two most-prescribed forms of medication in our country today are painkillers and antidepressants?

How is it that, in the richest, most well-resourced country the world has ever known with the best defense the world has ever produced, the National Institute for Mental Health reports a third of us will suffer from an anxiety disorder in our lifetimes?

How is it that according to the American Psychological Association, 38 percent of adults admit to turning to food to combat stress?

How is it that we can connect to 1.1 billion people through Facebook, and yet 60 percent of people told *TIME* magazine they feel worse after spending time on social media?

We are the richest nation the world has ever known—yes, but we are also a massively in debt, habitually addicted, and a chronically hurried and worried nation.

Is it possible to have everything yet possess nothing?

Is it possible to work hard to strive for a lifestyle our world tells us we need and come to a realization that you don't possess that life, *but it possesses you?*

And when we do that, we reverse the words of Scripture over us.

We have resigned ourselves to living behind a false painting bound by deceptive frames, and people think it is the genuine article. Our true and most authentic selves are unknown, yet we are regarded as known. We live on, yet we are dying inside—we may not be dead yet, but we are beaten. People see the rejoicing façade outside, but we are sorrowful inside. We seem rich and our needs seem to have been met, but we feel poor, having everything and yet possessing nothing.

Maybe you have traded the masterpiece God created you to be for a poor, stained, inferior, dusty version of yourself—an old picture inside a rickety old frame worth four bucks at a flea market.

But if you have entrusted your life
to the One who sees the real you,
who has freed the real you,
who tears away the old picture,
who shatters every frame,
who destroys every chain that attempts to bind you,
who has declared the ultimate Declaration of Freedom,
then your life matters like crazy.

And if we pause long enough to listen closely to our soul's cry, something inside of us is telling us this is true.

Chapter 4

LONGING

*I*n the Gospel of Mark, a man comes running to Jesus and kneels before Him (Mark 10:17). This is not the way people behaved in the first-century Middle Eastern world. Grown men did not run like this. Luke calls him a ruler. He has status. He has wealth. But this man desperately wants to see Jesus. We see his passion—he not only runs to Jesus, he falls on his knees. He is showing a lot of respect to Jesus.

And he refers to Jesus as "good teacher." So this young man comes to Jesus and expresses his desire to learn about God and His purpose in an extraordinary way. He wants to know how he can be a part of God's kingdom.

Jesus replies, "You know the commandments: 'You shall not murder, you shall not commit adultery, you shall not steal, you shall not give false testimony, you shall not defraud, honor your father and mother'" (v. 19).

And he said to him, "Teacher . . . all these I have kept since I was a boy" (v. 20).

But we have to consider something about this young man. He had been very religious from the time he was just a boy. He religiously went to the synagogue, knew the Scriptures, kept the rules.

So then, why did he go to Jesus?

If he felt he had his relationship with God all taken care of and if he truly was following God's teachings closely and believed he did not break any of the commandments, why did he go to Jesus?

Some of the most common explanations among biblical scholars include that this young man wanted to be sure of his salvation, he was looking for approval, or he was just getting a second opinion.

Is it possible the reason goes a little deeper?

From a young age, he had been following a religion of doing, which is why he asked Jesus, *what must I do?* He was focused on his life, his achievements, his awards and trophies, his ability to make things happen. His life was preoccupied with himself.

He had come to believe in the frames and old paintings of religion and works. It had become such a part of him and his identity, he couldn't imagine his life without it.

He was following a religion of going through the motions, hitting the checklist, all the externals taken care of, but there was dissatisfaction in his soul.

Maybe he was starting to realize he had everything but in reality possessed nothing. He saw this man Jesus. He saw the people who hung around Jesus. They had nothing but seemed to possess everything.

I wonder if, deep in his soul, this young man had a longing, a sense that even with doing all the things he was doing, something was missing. All his wealth, all his stuff, all his achievements, all his knowledge about God, all his efforts to keep the law—his soul's longing could not be met that way. He had everything, but did he possess anything?

The cry of his soul had grown so intense that he ran to Jesus. Perhaps Jesus would have the answer.

Each and every one of us comes hardwired with this sense of longing. A sense that something is lacking, something is missing. This longing of the soul is not a desire for something; it is more than just desire, it is deeper than desire, it is a hunger of the soul.

Psalm 119:20 (NASB) says: "My soul is crushed with longing."

Frederick Buechner writes about this in his book, *The Longing for Home*:

Whether we're rich or poor, male or female . . . our stories are all stories of searching. We search for a good self to be and for good work to do. . . . We search to love and to be loved. And in a world where it is often hard to believe in much of anything, we search to believe in something holy and beautiful and life-transcending that will give meaning and purpose to the lives we live.

I think this resonates with a lot of people. All the rushing, all the accumulating, all the stuff, all the stress, and there is this sense, this longing we feel deep in our souls.

People are looking for something to live and die for. You see this play out in many ways. People moving constantly, hoping the next place will provide them the sense of belonging and acceptance they are looking for. Or they church hop or switch jobs. Or they try pleasure or alcohol or drugs or money or status or stuff. Trying to find an answer to their soul's deepest cry. Reaching for something just outside their grasp.

Some of the biggest music hits of all times are songs about a yearning. Track the highest grossing movies of all time, and you will see a theme of someone on a quest for something, trying to satisfy the longing of their souls.

> My soul longed and even yearned.
> —Psalm 84:2 NASB

Your soul has a longing.

But here's the problem. Here's the difficulty, the crisis, the predicament: The rich young man has wealth, he has status, he has impressive credentials, he has a lot of stuff. But none of that fulfils the deep longing of his soul.

Every human soul is born with this intense longing, and if you are a twenty-first-century American, you likely have resources, you have access to opportunities, you can exercise control, you have options.

And so people try to fill that longing with all sorts of things.

The part of Maryland where I live is considered one of the most affluent regions in the United States. While parents feel like they are giving their children the best opportunities, great schools, safe neighborhoods, and sports on weekends, we are seeing a dramatic rise of heroin addiction among teenagers in our region. Here's why—none of the other things, good as they may be, will fill a young person's deep sense of longing in their souls.

People try relationships, they try alcohol, they try drugs, they try sports, they try buying stuff, they try climbing the ladder at work, they try following rules for good living. And so we keep ourselves busy and stressed and rushed and distracted from the call of our soul's cry.

So here is this young man who sought out Jesus: He's notched up an impressive résumé at a very young age. He is young. He is rich. He has status. He is part of the upper class in society. He is successful. None of it seemed to satisfy the call of his soul's deepest cry. So he comes to Jesus thinking maybe Jesus has the answer to his soul's deepest longings.

There is a beautiful phrase the writer inserts at this point of the story, and I think this is critical to our understanding this account, "And Jesus, looking at him, loved him" (Mark 10:21 ESV).

Jesus feels a deep love for this young man. He sees the tremendous potential of this young man. Jesus loved the young man for who he is and for who he could become.

Mark continues, "And Jesus, looking at him, loved him, and said to him, 'You lack one thing: go, sell all that you have and give to the poor, and you will have treasure in heaven; and come, follow me.'"

Some people think this commandment is for all followers of Jesus. And people can get hung up on this point of the story. This commandment is not for all believers. There's a very simple way to explain this. Jesus doesn't tell others to do the same thing.

So, why this young man?

Jesus can see what's going on at the soul level for this young man. His soul has a longing. Jesus knows about that longing. It's hardwired into the human soul. But his soul is in the grip of stuff. And it doesn't satisfy. He knows it. Jesus knows it. Only Jesus can take that place.

The young man listens to Jesus. He doesn't say a word. He probably looks at the disciples standing near Jesus. They have nothing, or so he thinks. "Disheartened by the saying, he went away sorrowful, for he had great possessions" (v. 22 ESV).

He was disheartened and sorrowful because he had great possessions. The bottom line is this: A soul that seeks after God but says no to God will always be dejected and discouraged. The longing in our souls is designed to call us to our most authentic selves as revealed in the masterpiece God has created us to be. Encountering Jesus will mean having to face the old paintings and frames that hide the real masterpiece. However, we are granted the freedom to allow Jesus to rip off the old, dusty painting and frames or choose to keep them as a ragged veil hiding a priceless treasure.

This young man had the chance to have the longing of his soul fulfilled, to be the masterpiece God created him to be, but he chose not to.

I can tell you, he probably remained disheartened and sorrowful. A soul that seeks after God but says no to God will always be dejected and discouraged. There is no satisfaction for the human soul remaining behind the veil of a dusty fake.

The longing of our souls is to find Someone who can remove the old painting and frames from our lives.

We need Someone who has the power and strength and wisdom to guide us to be the person we were created to be so that our soul's true image and character and life can be revealed as the masterpiece it was meant to be. And unless that happens, we remain trapped in our past, behind the dusty, old painting and the rickety, old frames.

Chapter 5

PAST—1

*L*ike everyone, you have a past. You have had your share of joys and pains, successes and setbacks, ups and downs. Then there are things you are not proud of—decisions you are remorseful for, words and actions you regret—your sins.

You are not alone.

No one is.

For some of us, our sin is more obvious—plain as daylight for all to see.

And it shrouds and obscures and masks the masterpiece in a dismal, dusty, discolored, damaged, disgraced disguise.

The good news is there is Someone who can rip apart the veil of sinful choices, decisions, words, and actions from our lives. It has happened for millions of people through the ages.

It can happen for you. It can only happen if you stop long enough to have a chat with the Creator of the masterpiece, which is what happened one day in Samaria.

Jesus and His disciples were on a journey. Jesus was a poor man. So he was walking with His disciples. As recorded in John 4, He comes to a town in Samaria around noon. He sits down by a well while His disciples go to town to get food. Jesus is fully God, but Jesus is also fully man. He gets tired. He gets hungry. He gets thirsty. And so here He is.

John captures the scene this way: "When a Samaritan woman came to draw water, Jesus said to her, 'Will you give me a drink?' (His disciples had gone into the town to buy food)" (vv. 7–8).

Jesus asks her for a drink.

What an extraordinarily dramatic and stunning scene!

The God who created the oceans, the lakes, and the rivers is thirsty and is asking a woman He created for a drink!

Biblical scholars and commentators have written a lot about this conversation. (If you want to see this familiar story with fresh eyes, read chapter 15 of the excellent book, *Jesus Through Middle Eastern Eyes* by Kenneth Bailey. It is a brilliant and engrossing book.) The woman is all alone. She is a Samaritan woman, a member of a group of people who were despised and shunned by the Jews. No respectable Jewish rabbi would have talked to a Samaritan woman.

The woman is taken aback. A Jewish man talking to a Samaritan woman would have been remarkable. That He would actually ask for a drink *from her bucket* would have been scandalous.

She responds by asking Him how *He* could ask *her* for a drink. Jesus tells her, "If you knew the gift of God and who it is that asks you for a drink, you would have asked him and he would have given you living water" (v. 10).

She responds by asking Him for that water so she wouldn't have to make the daily trip to the well.

Jesus points her to the fact that God is now here, dwelling among them. The woman wants a religion that will satisfy her immediate needs, her pain, her discomfort. A religion that will save her from making this solitary, painful, sad trip to the well day in and day out. Could it be that . . .

Every step to and from the well reminds her of her past?

Every step to and from the well reminds her of all the mistakes she has made?

Every step to and from the well reminds her of the choices she feels guilty about, decisions she is remorseful for, words and actions she regrets?

Every step to and from the well reminds her of the despair and desperation of her life's circumstances?

Every step reminds her no one will associate with her, be friends with her, walk with her?

Every step reminds her of how little her life is worth?

Rickety, old frames of her past decisions, failed relationships, shattered reputation, and broken promises bind her identity.

So, she says, "Sir, give me that water so that I don't have to take this painful, lonely, wretched trip any more. I am done with this."

Then the story takes a dramatic turn. Jesus confronts her sin, her darkness, her past with grace and truth.

Here is a sad life. A lonely life. A hurting life. A life covered up by a dusty, grimy, faded, old painting trapped in a rickety, old frame of her past and her sins. And it shrouds and obscures and masks the masterpiece in a dismal, dusty, discolored, damaged, disgraced disguise.

She needs Someone who can rip apart the sins of past choices and decisions and words and actions from her life. A life that has never experienced truth and grace and love, and here comes God in flesh to have this one-on-one conversation with her. He sits down with her and devotes a lot of time to her.

Interestingly, she tries to hide behind the frame.

Because Jesus is the Creator of the masterpiece, it cannot be hidden from Him. So He sees, understands, notices, and perceives what is going on inside her.

Jesus knows who we are, and He knows our past and our sin and our regrets and our guilt. He knows when we are thirsty and weary. He knows when we are in pain and in trouble. He knows the exact nature of the junk of our past choices. He knows when we hold on to our pride, our sin, our self-righteousness. He is familiar with all our ways.

He knows.

Jesus Christ came not to condemn you but to save you, knowing your name, knowing all about you . . . He knows you individually as though there were not another person in the entire

world. He died for you as certainly as if you had been the only lost one. He knows the worst about you and is the One who loves you the most.

–A. W. Tozer, *And He Dwelt Among Us*

What we do not understand sometimes is that we are not strong enough to tear down the old paintings and frames of our past and our sins. That doesn't stop us from trying!

We hear this, and at some conceptual level understand this but keep reverting back to trying to do this on our own.

This happens a lot with the followers of Jesus Christ. People react to this in a few ways.

Some of us start to think, *I need to try harder, maybe do things that are hard and make me miserable, especially when I sin or stumble or am going through a tough season in my life.*

Or we start thinking, *I will keep up appearances. Inside, I am struggling with doubts, pain, and hurts no one knows, but I will just pretend and continue this journey with Jesus in His community. I will go through the motions and say the right things, do the right things when others are watching. Maybe that is the answer.* When sin remains unconfessed, secrets remain safe, but transformation remains elusive. Some of us are doing this right now and are slowly dying inside.

Or we start getting legalistic. *If I can keep the rules, read the Word, pray for a certain amount of time, that should do it.* And of course, then we start to feel guilty when we fail.

Or we just become discouraged. We start thinking, *I will never be the masterpiece God created me to be—I just have so many issues, so much baggage, my sins are so terrible, maybe even God has given up on me.* We get discouraged.

If you are going through a tough season, becoming a masterpiece for God seems like a cruel joke, a cosmic hoax, or an unattainable religious tenet.

But Jesus insists He can do this for you if you allow Him.

I want to take a moment and specifically address anyone who feels despair, pain, failure, weakness, or helpless about past sins and decisions and choices. And I want to do that by taking you to a festival.

John 7:37 begins the story, "On the last and greatest day of the festival, Jesus stood and said in a loud voice."

To understand what Jesus is saying, we need to understand the context. The text says it was the last and greatest day of the festival.

On the Hebrew calendar, there were several major feasts. You can find an executive summary of these feasts in Leviticus 23. They were arranged mostly around agriculture—planting and harvesting and so on. There were feasts held in spring, and then there were feasts held during the autumn when the harvesting would be done.

The feast in John 7 is the last major feast of the year—the Feast of Tabernacles. The idea was similar to the way we celebrate Thanksgiving, except the people would gather in tents for a week. This was to remind them how they used to live in the wilderness and how God cared for them.

The celebration would last for several days. During this feast, there was singing and rituals that centered on thanking God and also praying for rain for their crops the following year. As you can imagine, the theme of water played a prominent role in this festival.

The highlight of the festival was at the end of the feast, on the last day, when the priest would take a container full of water and pour it out as a celebration of when God provided water from a rock in the desert for His people (Exodus 17). And the people would shout and cheer. Some would yell, "Hosanna, Hosanna!" which means "save" or "God, save us."

Now in the midst of all this teaching about water, ritual of pouring out water on the last day of the festival, and celebration of thanksgiving, prayer, and praising God for rain and water, Jesus stands up and says these words: "Let anyone who is thirsty come to me and drink" (John 7:37).

People around Him are focusing on the ritual, the feast, the festival, the thanksgiving, the pouring of water, the thanking of a God who satisfied their thirst, and Jesus stands there, right in the middle of all that, and says there is such a thing as spiritual thirst, and He can provide the Living Water to take care of it.

What is Jesus really saying? What does this passage mean for us today?

Jesus is saying if you are thirsty, He can help. If your soul is thirsty and you are tired of the old paintings and frames of sin and regret, He can forgive and restore and redeem you.

You realize you are thirsty, and God is willing to meet you right there, in the middle of your thirst, your mess, and your need and accept you just as you are but not leave you as you are. This God, who became flesh sees the thirst of our souls and offers Living Water. He offers to rip apart the frames of our past, of our sins, of our guilt, and reveal our soul's truest identity and give it its deepest meaning.

Sometimes people simply give up. Because of life experiences, toxic beliefs, or intense discouragement, some simply walk away. When we choose to walk away or stay hidden behind old paintings and frames, we start to think and believe that God has rejected us.

God hasn't rejected us. We have rejected Him. And by rejecting Him, we have rejected our true and real selves.

Chapter 6

PAST—2

Maybe you have already allowed Jesus to enter your life as your Lord and Savior, confessed your sins, and received His forgiveness. You thought life was going to go a certain way, but then it didn't.

Circumstances came your way that were not caused by you, and you became the recipient of some tragic news or some heartbreaking experiences. You got hurt badly. Maybe you got labeled and abused, and now you feel wounded and bruised and betrayed and wonder, *How do I gather the pieces of my life and begin again?* There is a story of a woman who endured many years under the burden of old, rickety, ugly, dirty, filthy frames of labels and hurt and rejection. She used all her resources. She tried hard. But nothing worked. She needed to face her Creator to help reveal her true worth, her true identity, the masterpiece she was created to be. More on that in a moment.

A guy by the name of Bill Tancer wrote an interesting book called *Click: What Millions of People Are Doing Online and Why It Matters*. Tancer is a global research manager and an expert on online behavior. Through his online market research firm, he monitors the daily online behavior of more than 10 million Internet users. In other words, none of our googling and yahooing is private (you knew that, right?). This guy has been studying it for years. And his book contains some pretty surprising insights.

One part of his research uncovered that when people are surveyed about their top fears or phobias face-to-face or over the phone, three of the top phobias are almost always the same: rodents, heights, and water.

Tancer then researched the various fears people searched on the Internet. In other words, he was curious to see if people search for the same fears when doing the searches privately as opposed to answering a phone or live surveyor. He found online search topics varied greatly from the offline surveys. In other words, in the privacy of online searches, people were much more open to sharing their deepest fears.

According to Tancer's research, Americans' biggest fears, as evidenced by online searches, relate to intimacy and rejection.

It seems like a lot of people struggle with a sense of their core identity. Is my life worth more than a flea market item? They are carrying paintings and frames of what the world tells them and puts on them. And some have been rejected so many times, they are fearful of it.

Some time back, my wife, Erika, was out with three of our four girls, and I was home alone with Ayanna, my then six-year-old. It was lunchtime, so I looked in the refrigerator and took out some leftover Indian food Erika made the night before. I heated it up in the microwave, set the table, and called to Ayanna to join me for lunch. As I started putting out the food, Ayanna looked at the meal and said, "Dad, I don't want to eat Indian food."

I asked her why not.

She said, "Because I don't like Indian food."

So I said, "Well, you know your dad was born and grew up in India, so you really should like Indian food."

She replied, "No, Dad, I don't like Indian food because I am not an Indian."

So I looked her in the eyes and said, "OK, you are not an Indian. Who are you? And what are you doing in my house?"

And she replied, "I am a kid, Dad."

So I said, "What does that have to do with food?"

And she replied, "I am a kid, that's why I don't like Indian food. I like kid food."

I asked, "And can you give me some examples of kid food that I can serve you?"

And she replied, "Sure, you can give me kid food like cheese, chocolate, and candy."

Of course, she didn't get kid food. We had an interesting and contentious discussion about our roles and who she is.

The essence of what I said to her was this: "You are my daughter, and I am your father. That is who you are, and I, as your father, know what kind of food is best for you—food that is good for you, nutritious for you, and that will make you grow—not junk food but healthy food."

It is my job as Ayanna's dad to make sure she understands what her real identity is, what the real masterpiece Jesus created her to be looks like. If I allow her to think that the most important factor defining her is that she is a kid or whatever label she or the world throws at her, she will hunger after things that are defined by that identity.

But if I help her understand—

**that I see her as someone
who is creative, sensitive, compassionate, generous,
inspired, committed, authentic, energetic, giving, playful,
inquisitive, wise, nurturing, feminine, and loving;**

**that she is a daughter of the living God,
loved deeply and unconditionally by her heavenly Father
and her earthly father and mother;
that God created her to be an exceptional woman someday—**

**if she grows up knowing this is who she is,
then she will hunger after the things defined by that identity.**

A lot of us struggle with this. A lot of people in our world are walking around with a warped and distorted and damaged old painting of themselves, and so they say things and do things that are defined by this distorted sense of identity derived from that painting.

A distorted sense of identity can produce shame and confusion.

A human soul in the grip of shame does terrible things to the identity of a person.

Shame is different than guilt. One distinction I have heard is that we feel guilty for what we have done, but we feel shame for who we think we are.

Experts who study shame tell us that a human soul battling shame can display all kinds of behaviors such as addiction, hopelessness, eating disorders, violence, bullying, and anger.

Shame can be deadly. It goes deep into your soul, often defining the person you are, robbing you of your true identity. Shame is a powerful veil that covers the real masterpiece. Shame will destroy your sense of self-worth. It will sap your spirit. It can kill relationships. It can drive people to isolation and despair.

And this is what happened to the woman in our story.

It has been a busy day for Jesus. Crowds are waiting for Jesus. They have needs. Among them is Jairus, a spiritual leader. He comes to Jesus and falls at His feet. He begs Jesus to come with him and heal his 12-year-old daughter who is very sick. As I am writing this, I have a 12-year-old daughter. I can feel Jairus's pain. I would do anything for my girl.

Mark tells the story this way: "So Jesus went with him. A large crowd followed and pressed around him" (Mark 5:24).

Jesus is going to Jairus's house, and the crowds are all pressing in around Him. That's the context. So here's what happens next.

"And a woman was there who had been subject to bleeding for twelve years. She had suffered a great deal under the care of many doctors and had spent all she had, yet instead of getting better she grew worse" (vv. 25–26).

Maybe you know the pain of this. When you go from doctor to doctor, and none of them can seem to diagnose the real issue, all while you spend time and money.

This woman's pain is a private one. Her anguish is real. Her resources are gone, and her hope is waning. Her condition has likely left her weak and anemic. No one is with her. We don't even know her name; we know her by her illness. We get the sense that from the world's perspective, this is an insignificant, unwanted, shunned woman.

But she had heard about Jesus. Maybe she had heard that Jesus was compassionate toward the poor, the sick, and the destitute. She had lived with this oppressive, old painting and restrictive frame for the past 12 years. Maybe Jesus could rip it apart.

"When she heard about Jesus, she came up behind him in the crowd and touched his cloak, because she thought, 'If I just touch his clothes, I will be healed'" (vv. 27–28).

She doesn't come and fall at the feet of Jesus like Jairus, but comes behind Jesus, secretly. Why?

Under the Mosaic Law (as recorded in Leviticus 15), a woman having a flow of blood was considered unclean, which meant that anything she touched was unclean. If she sat on something, it was considered unclean. If she touched someone, that person became unclean. As long as the flow of blood was there, she was unclean.

For 12 long years, she has been unclean. It is not something she could hide. The shame of this old painting and frame was upon her. It was her identity, her title, her status—she was unclean. If she were married, she couldn't even touch her husband without making him unclean. Or her children. Or her neighbors and friends.

For 12 long years, she was likely living a very lonely, isolated, hopeless life. She knows what it means to be unwanted and rejected.

The masterpiece within was shrouded and covered up with a cheap painting titled *Unclean*.

But she hears that Someone is in town who has performed miracles and brought hope to the hopeless. Maybe He can rip apart the old frames and painting of shame from her life. Maybe He can restore and redeem her to reveal the masterpiece she was created to be. Maybe He has the power to do this. Maybe He will have compassion upon her and help her.

But everyone knows and sees her for the old painting and frame of shame she has carried for so long. She can't possibly walk in the middle of the crowd and reach out to Jesus. People know she is Ms. Unclean.

Some of us know about this. Maybe it is not something you did, but circumstances came about that cast a shroud of dust and grime over your life, obscuring the masterpiece God wants you to be.

Perhaps early on in life, you were told you were not good enough, smart enough, or attractive enough. Perhaps someone you loved walked out of your life. Perhaps there were life experiences that sucked the joy and life and hope out of you. And you wake up every morning, and an invisible hand puts on a fresh brushstroke of shame upon you. You carry it quietly, secretly even. And you have carried this fake painting for way too long. And that fake painting has come to define your soul, your identity, and your very existence.

There are only two ways to deal with the fake painting of past shame. One way is to continue in isolation, secrecy, and hiding. The woman in our story has carried this fake painting upon her for 12 years. She has come to believe she is flea market material. Then, one day, all that changes.

She sneaks up on Jesus and touches the hem of His garment.

Immediately her bleeding stopped and she felt in her body that she was freed from her suffering. At once Jesus realized that power had gone out from him. He turned around in the crowd and asked, "Who

touched my clothes?" "You see the people crowding against you," his disciples answered, "and yet you can ask, 'Who touched me?'" But Jesus kept looking around to see who had done it. Then the woman, knowing what had happened to her, came and fell at his feet and, trembling with fear, told him the whole truth.

—Mark 5:29–33

Under Mosaic Law, by touching Jesus, this woman would actually make Jesus unclean. She is ashamed. She is scared. She is trembling.

We live in a society that shuns shame in favor of pretense. But pretense is not real. It is a flimsy veil with which we try to cover our shame. And this veil restricts the light of recovery and restoration to filter through and bring healing.

So we try and deal with this privately. Like the woman in our story, we carry the old paintings and frames of shame, regret, hurt, and the pain of our past.

One way is to continue in isolation, secrecy, and hiding. The other way is to find Someone who can rip that old, dusty, grimy painting and frame of shame apart. And reveal to us what our true identity, the true masterpiece, looks like. We can hide and try to fix it on our own, or we can come to the Master and be transformed—those are the only two ways to handle shame.

And Jesus turns around and looks for this woman.

Jesus looks for you. Jesus looks for me. He looks at all the filthy, dirty, grimy, dusty, fake paintings, and He longs to rip them apart.

The woman is trembling. She is afraid Jesus will be angry and upset. She is afraid by coming to Jesus she has perhaps made Him unclean. But because He is pure and sinless Savior, He doesn't become unclean. She becomes clean! Such is the power of transformation. It is a new day for her. And Jesus, who kept looking for her, is about to reveal to her the true masterpiece she was created to be.

When the woman finishes telling her painful, heartbreaking story, Jesus says to her, "Daughter, your faith has healed you. Go in peace and be freed from your suffering" (v. 34).

What a lovely, life-giving, soul-shaping statement.

For 12 years, this woman has had to bear the dusty, grimy painting and the old, rickety frames that showed the world she was an outcast, she didn't belong, she was unwanted and unclean—a flea market item.

That day, everything changed. In one sweeping gesture, Jesus revealed the masterpiece of her life. Not only has the old painting and frame been ripped apart, but the title of *Unclean* has been erased. Jesus put a new title on the masterpiece of her life—*daughter!*

For 12 long years, she was unclean. She couldn't touch, she couldn't enter homes, and she couldn't even be around people. But that day, she could touch and hug and eat and be part of a community. That day, she could be a masterpiece.

This is the only time in the Gospels that Jesus referred to someone as *daughter*. Jesus was saying, "You don't have to carry this burden of old paintings and frames and shame anymore. I am ripping off all the labels and frames and paintings people gave you. I am tearing away all the junk identity and giving you a new identity. Daughter! You are now part of my family, my community. 'Your faith has healed you.'" Not only is she physically healed, she now has a relationship with the Creator of the masterpiece of her life.

Brennan Manning writes in *Abba's Child*, "Define yourself radically as one beloved of God. This is the true self. Every other identity is an illusion."

More than anything, this woman needs to understand that she is beloved of God. Jesus calls her daughter. More than anything, you need to know, you are beloved of God. You are His child.

The only way you can break apart the old paintings and frames of shame, of sin, of despair, is through the grace of God offered to us through the finished work of our Lord Jesus Christ, His life, His death, His Resurrection.

Hebrews 12:2 (NASB) tells us, "fixing our eyes on Jesus, the author and perfecter of faith, who for the joy set before Him endured the cross, despising the shame." And because of this, Jesus can rip apart our old paintings and frames of sin and shame and reveal the true masterpiece that gives us the identity, and the love, and the security and the protection our souls crave.

Chapter 7

SPARK

*I*f you look at the lives of people who are doing great work, who are living in a way that is in sync with the masterpiece they were created to be, you will find it often starts with a spark—*that defining moment when the human soul rises above the mundane, the routine, the buzz of everyday life and catches a glimpse of what a true masterpiece could be.*

Whether it is a life dedicated to impacting a few or millions is not the issue (more on that in the next section). We are talking about connecting with your soul's deepest impulse.

And it often starts with a spark—a need you see, a book you read, a sermon you hear, a conversation with which you engage. And something—a word or a phrase or a story or a verse or a metaphor—slams right through the carefully crafted existence of modern life and touches a nerve. It annoyingly pricks at your heart. It frustratingly rattles around in your head. It maddeningly messes with your soul. And you just can't seem to get rid of it.

That's when you know you have to do something about it. That's the definition of a soul spark.

It happened to Matthew, the tax collector. It happened to Peter and John. It happened to Mary and Martha. It happened to Paul. It happened to Martin Luther. It happened to Martin Luther King Jr. It happened to Mother Teresa. It happened to Billy Graham. It has happened and continues to happen to millions.

A spark that ignites the human soul.

It happened to Favio Chávez one day.

Favio is from the country of Paraguay. In 2006, Favio got a job at the huge government trash and recycle program in Catuera—a slum built upon a landfill where approximately 1,500 tons of solid waste are dumped every single day. About 2,500 families live in Catuera and rely on their jobs of recycling or sorting through trash at the landfill as their main source of income. The town is so saturated with stench and garbage that every time it rains, the town is flooded with contaminated water.

In the middle of all this are kids growing up in slums with very little opportunity. For many of them, their career is sealed into working at the country's largest garbage dump.

Favio could have settled into his job and lived relatively comfortably, but instead he decided to do something. He decided to give the children of the slum the gift of music. As a child, he had taken music lessons and even became the choir director at his church at the age of 11.

He started teaching kids how to play classical music, but he soon realized his increasing number of pupils would need to practice at home if they would ever progress as musicians. And when the price of a violin is more than the price of a house in Catuera, Favio had to get creative.

He roped in a friend, Nicolás Gómez, and together they started making cellos, drums, violins, and flutes out of trash—metal oven trays, oil barrels, forks, and old strips of wood.

Favio began his lessons with 50 students. Today, his program has grown to more than 250 students a year. Now, the slums of Catuera fill up with music as Favio passionately, lovingly, and persistently teaches these kids.

They call themselves the Recycled Orchestra. A few years ago, a filmmaker heard their story and raised funds through the online crowdfunding platform Kickstarter to make a documentary. (Check it out at landfillharmonicmovie.com.)

This put them on the map. All of a sudden, these kids led by Favio were getting invitations from around the world.

When asked what got him started, Favio says, "People realize that we shouldn't throw away trash carelessly. Well, we shouldn't throw away people either."

If you look at people who are making a difference like Favio Chavéz, you will find one common denominator—there is a moment in their lives when there was a spark.

People have called it all sorts of things—halftime, a conversion experience, an epiphany—but I think it's more than that.

It's an illuminating moment, a spark for the soul. It is the precursor to peeling back the mundane old painting and frames and revealing the masterpiece within.

You can try to stifle this sense, you can try to deaden it, disown it, drown it, but it never really goes away.

You may be pursuing the American dream. Life may not be all rosy or perfect, but you've got a house. Maybe you are single, maybe you are married, you have a car, you have a good job, or you have at least some retirement savings.

You never go to bed hungry, you never have to worry about having clothing to wear, you never have to worry about being without a roof over your head. Life is steadily, comfortably, peacefully moving along. But there is this tugging at your soul—a tiny, flickering bulb in your consciousness that keeps nudging you, jolting you, even irritating you—to take the risk of allowing God to reveal the masterpiece God created you to be.

I believe it happened for Favio Chavéz one day, and I believe it can happen for you.

This spark is designed to guide us to find Someone who can help us identify and reveal the masterpiece we were created to be. But the first step is up to us. We have been given the freedom to choose. Remain behind fake paintings and frames or take the risk and become the masterpiece we were created to be.

And that first step starts with the spark. This unrelenting impulse in our soul that refuses to go away. It is telling us something.

If that hasn't happened for you, maybe you need to pause and listen. In an interview, theologian Frederick Buechner was asked how to listen to our souls. His answer is brilliant and thoughtful and could be the first step to discovering your spark. Apart from your primary resource of time in the Bible and prayer, listen to Buechner's words:

Try this. Keep track of any event in the course of a week, a month, a year, that brings tears to your eyes. They may be happy moments or sad moments or moments that on the surface seem quite unremarkable, but in whichever case they are moments when you have been stirred to your roots, and it is there, at your roots, that God is at work in your life. Examine those moments with great care, ask why they brought tears, and you will learn much about God and about yourself too.

PICTURE

The great Christian revolutions come not by the discovery of something that was not known before. They happen when someone takes radically something that was always there.

—H. Richard Niebuhr

Chapter 8

BIRTH

*I*n November 2003, our second daughter Ashlynne was born. I had gone through this before with our firstborn, Elizabeth, so I thought I was brave enough and tough enough to go through the birth of another baby.

We arrived at the hospital, and after a few hours the doctor came in and said they would have to do an emergency C-section due to some complications. They wheeled in my wife, Erika, and I went with her, feeling quite sick in my stomach. In the surgery room, they had a dividing curtain, and I was sitting next to Erika and assuring her everything was going to be all right.

Actually what I was thinking was, *Lord, please give me enough strength to get through this.* A few minutes into the process, my curiosity got the better of me, and I peeked over the curtain to see what they were doing. All I saw was Ashlynne's blood-soaked face emerging from Erika's stomach.

The next thing I remember is tapping the nurse next to me and saying, "I think I am going to faint." The nurse directed me to go to the adjoining room.

And I looked at Erika and said, "Don't worry, honey, I'll be back soon." I was half-unconscious, and they made me sit down in the next room and pointed a huge fan at me.

Sometime later I remember holding Ashlynne in my hands— this beautiful little girl God had blessed us with.

Five years later, we had our third daughter, Ayanna.

In some hospitals a pregnant woman is allowed to have up to

two people in the operation theater with her during her C-section. So before Ayanna's delivery date, Erika sat down with me and said very kindly, "Raj, do you think you will faint again?"

I said, "I'll try not to."

She said, "Just to be safe, I want to invite one of my friends to be in there with me."

So our friend Jennifer Maier was in the delivery room when Ayanna was born.

And I am proud to say I did not faint, although I very much felt like I wanted to.

The birth of a child is an amazing thing. So many doctors and specialists checked in on her in the days right after Ayanna was born. And then came our fourth child, Amber. What a blessing these four daughters are to me and their mother.

I applied for a birth certificate for each of them. The birth certificate and hospital records tell me a lot about my kids:

What was the baby's weight?

What was her length?

What was her eye color?

What was her body temperature?

What was the exact time my child was born?

Who are her parents?

But it doesn't answer these questions:

Why was she born?

What is the purpose of her life?

What is she meant to do with the gift of this one and only life?

What is going to be her story?

It doesn't answer these questions.

These are not just questions of preeminent importance for Elizabeth, Ashlynne, Ayanna, and Amber, my four girls. These are questions for each and every one of us.

So then, who is best equipped to answer these questions? The world will try and put its own spin on these questions. Philosophers, thinkers, friends, family members, and others will try and come up with answers for us. Sometimes, we think we can make our own answers for these questions. Unfortunately, *all of these answers end up becoming like the old paintings and frames, hiding the real you, the authentic you, the masterpiece you.*

If you want to know the purpose and function of your car, you look at its manufacturer. If you want to know the purpose and function of your iPhone, you contact Apple. If you want to know the purpose and function of anything, you will likely turn to its maker.

It would seem the creator of something should have the best information on the purpose and function of its creation. Therefore, if we want to know the purpose and function of the human soul, we have to turn to its Creator.

The great Bible commentator, William Barclay, once wrote:

It frequently happens that the value of a thing lies in the fact that someone has possessed it. A very ordinary thing acquires a new value if some famous person has possessed it. In any museum we will find quite ordinary things–clothes, a walking-stick, a pen, books, pieces of furniture–which are of value only because they were once possessed by some great person. It is the same with the Christians. Christians may be very ordinary people, but they acquire a new value because they belong to God.

Barclay insists that our greatness as Christians lies in the fact that we belong to God.

In other words, ownership determines worth.

The Bible says God created the human soul.

And the LORD God formed man of the dust of the ground, and breathed into his nostrils the breath of life; and man became a living soul.

—Genesis 2:7 KJV

Even every one that is called by my name: for I have created him for my glory, I have formed him; yea, I have made him.

—Isaiah 43:7 KJV

For in him all things were created: things in heaven and on earth, visible and invisible, whether thrones or powers or rulers or authorities; all things have been created through him and for him.

—Colossians 1:16

Created through Him? For Him?

The theme is found throughout the Bible.

The LORD has made everything for his own purposes.

—Proverbs 16:4 NLT

This brings us back to the text we started with, the foundation for this book:

For we are God's masterpiece. He has created us anew in Christ Jesus, so we can do the good things he planned for us long ago.

—Ephesians 2:10 NLT

To understand the purpose of the masterpiece, we have to start here—with the created and Creator part. Only then can we learn how to become the masterpiece our soul yearns for and longs for and was created for.

Chapter 9

GOD

You are God's masterpiece. You are not your own masterpiece. Therefore, before we can talk further about the masterpiece, we have to settle the matter about God. Specifically, whom we think God really is.

Your understanding of God massively influences your understanding of the masterpiece of you.

When you look at the word at the top of this page, what images come to your mind?

How do you view God?

Who is God?

What is God like?

Is God an angry God ready to throw natural disasters and lob all sorts of judgmental catastrophes on people, especially those He doesn't like?

Is God authoritarian? Judgmental?

Does God revel in giving out harsh punishments? Does He enjoy making people suffer?

Or is God benevolent, generous, and accommodating?

Or is God critical, reserved, and distant?

ABC News ran a story about the four ways Americans view God, based on the book *America's Four Gods* by Paul Froese and Christopher Bader. Just over a quarter of Americans believe God is authoritarian and judgmental. God is angry, angry at our sins, angry at the way we are managing our affairs in this life and in our world.

Another quarter believes in a benevolent God who is loving, not stern. He is very forgiving and warm. He is like the father of the prodigal son. He is the God that gives us second chances. He is deeply involved but is more inclined to bless rather than judge and punish.

About 16 percent of us believe in a critical God. He is powerful and is unhappy and disheartened at us humans. There is coming a day when He will exact His judgment.

And just under a quarter of us believe in a distant God. He made the world, but then became distant and disengaged. He is cosmic force that is less inclined to interact intimately or personally with us humans.

Authoritarian God?
Benevolent God?
Critical God?
Distant God?
What is God like?

Is God cranky and enraged? A divine policeman who watches and waits, ready to trounce anyone deviating from His rules?

Is God warm and gentle? A grandfather-type person full of love and mercy but no judgment?

Is God a nitpicker? A hypercritical superdad, who constantly tells us how we fall short? Picking up on our slightest mistakes, sins, and stumbles?

Is God simply distant and disengaged? A superbeing who created the universe, left it spinning, and then sort of moved away and watches us from a distance? He is just there looking, watching, but not really engaged with what's going on in our world.

Who is God?

Author Paul Froese is a professor at Baylor University. His research inspired the ABC News story, and he was quoted, "A person's conception of God is central to how they perceive their world and behave in it."

Let's take a moment to let that sink in: *a person's conception of God is central to how they perceive their world and behave in it.*

I believe Froese is right. And that's why the right view of God is very, very important, and we need to settle this before we can hope to be the masterpiece God created us to be. So what does the Bible say?

In the beginning God created all things, and all things were good. Very good. God saw all that He had made, and it was very good (Genesis 1:31).

God not only created us but made us in His own image, making us His image-bearers and giving us a calling to live in fellowship with Him and others. But then, because of the sin committed by the first couple God ever made, sin and darkness entered humanity. It disrupted and fractured our relationship with God and with each other. We became a people desperately in need of redemption and healing.

God did not abandon His creation and us. Throughout Scripture, His goal has been restoration. God's plan of restoration reached a climax through His Son Jesus. "And the Word became flesh and dwelt among us, and we beheld His glory"(John 1:14 NKJV). Or as *The Message* translates it, "The Word became flesh and blood, and moved into the neighborhood."

The Word became flesh?
God became human?
The Word that formed the Himalayas, the Pacific Ocean,
The Milky Way,
The sun, the moon, the stars,
The land creatures and the sea creatures.
The planets, the black holes, and the comets,

That Word
Became one of us?

Not anywhere else in the universe,
Beyond the galaxies, distant, disengaged, disavowed,
But here on earth,
Dwelling among us,
Forming friendships with people He created,
Walking the earth He made,
Inhabiting the planet He tossed into space?

The Word became flesh and lived among us, with us, moved into our neighborhood. This is God in flesh—breathing, talking, walking, eating, sleeping, laughing, weeping, experiencing pain, sorrow, rejection, friendship, betrayal, and getting old. Before we can get to your story, we need to understand His story because it is His story that makes your story profound, meaningful, magnificent, and noble. It is the finished work of Jesus that makes the masterpiece of your life even possible.

What is God like?

If you have ever wondered, wrestled with that question, here's the answer—if you really want to know what God is like, then you need to look to Jesus.

Here's why. Because Scripture tell us:

In the beginning was the Word, and the Word was with God, and the Word was God. [Jesus] was with God in the beginning. Through [Jesus] all things were made; without [Jesus] nothing was made that has been made. In [Jesus] was life, and that life was the light of all mankind. . . . [Jesus] was in the world, and though the world was made through [Jesus], the world did not recognize him. Yet to all who did receive [Jesus], to those who believed in his name, he gave the right to become children of God.

—John 1:1–12

We all, like sheep, have gone astray, each of us has turned to our own way; and the LORD has laid on [Jesus] the iniquity of us all. [Jesus] was oppressed and afflicted, yet [Jesus] did not open his mouth; [Jesus] was led like a lamb to the slaughter, and as a sheep before its shearers is silent, so [Jesus] did not open his mouth.

—Isaiah 53:6–7

[Jesus] was despised and rejected by mankind, a man of suffering, and familiar with pain. . . . [Jesus] was pierced for our transgressions [for all the sinful, wrong things that we have ever said or done], [Jesus] was crushed for our iniquities; the punishment that brought us peace was on [Jesus], and by his wounds we are healed.

—Isaiah 53:3–5

[Jesus] is the image of the invisible God, the firstborn over all creation. For in [Jesus] all things were created [including you!]: things in heaven and on earth, visible and invisible, whether thrones or powers or rulers or authorities; all things have been created through [Jesus] and for [Jesus]. [You were created for Jesus. Hmmm. More on that later.] [Jesus] is before all things, and in [Jesus] all things hold together. And [Jesus] is the head of the body, the church; [Jesus] is the beginning and the firstborn from among the dead, so that in everything [Jesus] might have the supremacy. For God was pleased to have all his fullness dwell in [Jesus], and through [Jesus] to reconcile to himself all things, whether things on earth or things in heaven, by making peace through [Jesus'] blood, shed on the cross.

—Colossians 1:15–20

Jesus: Who, being in very nature God, did not consider equality with God something to be used to his own advantage; rather, [Jesus] made himself nothing by taking the very nature of a servant, being made in human likeness. And being found in appearance as a man, [Jesus] humbled himself by becoming obedient to death—even death on a cross! Therefore God exalted [Jesus] to the highest place and gave [Jesus] the name that is above every name, that at the name of Jesus every knee should bow, in heaven and on earth and under the earth, and every tongue acknowledge that Jesus Christ is Lord, to the glory of God the Father.

—Philippians 2:5–11

**Jesus is the Son of God, yes, and
He is also the Wisdom of God.
He is the Power of God.
He is the Image of God.
He is the Salvation of God.
He is the Everlasting God.
He is the Creator.**

He is the Sustainer.

He is our Shepherd.

He is our Hope.

He is our King.

He is our Leader.

He is the Bread of Life.

He is the True Vine.

He is the Light of the world.

He is faithful and true and merciful and mighty.

He is the King of kings and the Lord of lords.

He is Lord of all.

He is the Lamb of God

Who takes away the sins of the world.

His name is Jesus.

And now, because of who Jesus is and what He has done,

Because Jesus became the Babe in the Manger,

Because Jesus became the Savior on the Cross,

Because Jesus became our Resurrected Lord,

If you believe this, then:

In Jesus, you are a child of God;

In Jesus, you are redeemed;

In Jesus, you are reconciled;

In Jesus, no weapon formed against you will prevail;

In Jesus, you are part of His church.

John Stott put it this way in his classic, *Basic Christianity*:

Many people visualize a God who sits comfortably on a distant throne, remote, aloof, uninterested and indifferent to the needs of mortals, until, it may be, they can badger him into taking action on their behalf. Such a view is wholly false. The Bible reveals a God who, long before it even occurs to us to turn to him, while we are still lost in darkness and sunk in sin, takes the initiative, rises from his throne, lays aside his glory and stoops to seek until we find him.

Paul says we are God's masterpiece, "created in Christ Jesus" (Ephesians 2:10). If we understand the created-in-Jesus part, we can then be ready to understand what that masterpiece really is. And how the created-for-Jesus part comes into play. This is so very important because your conception of God is central to how you perceive your world and behave in it.

A right relationship with God through Jesus is the starting point of you becoming the masterpiece God created you to be. To move from old paintings and frames of sin and shame to the new masterpiece we were created to be. From darkness to light. From death to life.

Chapter 10

DEATH TO LIFE

V irginia Woolf was a brilliant British author. Many people consider her to be one of the most significant literary voices of the first half of the twentieth century. She wrote many classic books and articles and essays. In 1942, a year after she died, one of her essays, "The Death of a Moth," was published.

One day, Woolf was reading by a window when a moth came flitting by and started to struggle. It began to lose its vitality and eventually died. She wrote about this experience in this essay:

It flashed upon me that he was in difficulties; he could no longer raise himself; his legs struggled vainly. . . . The body relaxed, and instantly grew stiff. The struggle was over. The insignificant little creature now knew death. As I looked at the dead moth, this minute wayside triumph of so great a force over so mean an antagonist filled me with wonder. . . . O yes, he seemed to say, death is stronger than I am.

It is a fascinating little essay and is considered by many to be one of the finest essays ever written. The question is why? Why does this piece of writing about the death of a moth still fascinate people? Why has this essay endured for more than seven decades?

What Virginia Woolf is saying is this: There is this amazing, vital bead of life that has been given to every creature, but there is a force, there is a power, there is this thing called death that is more powerful than life.

Death is coming. It is coming to each and every one of us. To every creature. And it is more powerful than life.

If you look, you will see evidence of death, decay, and degeneration all around you. The universe itself is slowing down. We see ourselves growing older, and signs of decay enter our personal space—shriveling skin, less hair, loss of memory. It's scary!

And some of us try to reverse or at least slow the process. People try all sorts of things—there are people who make billions of dollars saying you can actually cheat aging, decay, and death. People don't like the *D word*.

Some people believe death is the final act of life on earth. You die. Your story ends. You stop existing. It's the last period at the end of the book of your life. In the midst of this, Jesus comes and makes an astonishing statement. His words are stunning in their implications:

I tell you the truth, those who listen to my message and believe in God who sent me have eternal life. They will never be condemned for their sins, but they have already passed from death into life.

—John 5:24 NLT

In a world full of death, decay, and degeneration, Jesus makes an unusual and extraordinary promise—death to life!

What is this death Jesus is talking about here?

Sin has greatly distorted the masterpiece God created us to be. "For the wages of sin is death, but the gift of God is eternal life in Christ Jesus our Lord" (Romans 6:23). The effect of sin on the human soul is terminal. The Bible says this sin, this blot, the old paintings of all the wrong, horrible, hurtful things we have ever done, will result in death, eternal death.

Sin not only shrouds and conceals and dirties the masterpiece God created us to be but it also mangles and distorts and breaks and eventually destroys it.

This effect of sin is upon every human soul.
Every time we walk contrary to God and
don't care for the widows and orphans,
Don't feed the hungry or care for the sick,
Don't control our tongue,
Don't love our neighbors as ourselves.
Every time we give in to anger and arrogance
and vain arguments,
Every time we engage in boasting and
backbiting and bullying,
Every time we are prideful and lustful
and conceited and judgmental,
Every time we complain and condemn and curse and covet,
Every time we deceive and despise and defraud and disobey,
Every time we give in to jealousy and evil
and slander and greed and lies—
These are just some of the ways sin cloaks and subjugates
and disguises and defaces and scars the true masterpiece
God has created us to be.

We do not have the power to overcome, defeat, or remove the effect of sin from our souls by ourselves. Because God is both merciful and just, His justice required that a price be paid for our sins, for all our wrongdoing. There is a price tag attached to the removal of the old paintings and frames. We were incapable of paying that price. So God made a way in Jesus. Because of the life, death, and Resurrection of Jesus, we now have access to a way of being the masterpiece God created us to be. To be created anew in Christ Jesus. The word *anew* means "a new way or form that is unlike the previous one."

Our previous version was marred and scarred by sin. That was a life leading to death. But we were created anew in Christ to a life eternal. The masterpiece we were created to be in the first place.

Death to life!

And so, because of Jesus, we can experience life, life beyond death.

> When the perishable has been clothed with the imperishable, and the mortal with immortality, then the saying that is written will come true: "Death has been swallowed up in victory." "Where, O death, is your victory? Where, O death, is your sting?" The sting of death is sin, and the power of sin is the law. But thanks be to God! He gives us the victory through our Lord Jesus Christ.
>
> —1 Corinthians 15:54–57

Jesus is the only way to rip apart the old paintings and frames of sin and shame and regret and guilt from our lives and experience the life-giving power of God to turn us into the masterpiece He created us to be.

That life-giving power can be found in Jesus. He said:

> I am the way and the truth and the life. No one comes to the Father except through me.
>
> —John 14:6

I am the resurrection and the life. The one who believes in me will live, even though they die.

—John 11:25

I came so that everyone would have life, and have it in its fullest.

—John 10:10 CEV

God has given us eternal life, and this life is in his Son. Whoever has the Son has life; whoever does not have the Son of God does not have life.

—1 John 5:11–12

In his book *The Meaning of Marriage*, Tim Keller writes it this way:

The gospel is this: We are more sinful and flawed in ourselves than we ever dared believe, yet at the very same time we are more loved and accepted in Jesus Christ than we ever dared hope.

That is the gospel!

It is the paradigm-shifting, soul-shaping, life-giving good news that in the midst of a world filled with death, decay, and degeneration, in the midst of our darkest past and deepest thirst, our most awful sin, souls stained and scarred with old paintings and frames of sin and shame and guilt and regret, our futile attempts to earn our way out, our pitiful efforts to find our true and most authentic selves, God comes in and says, "I made you, I know you, I can redeem you. I can create you anew in Christ. I love you more than you'll ever know." It is not something we can earn or pay for. We can't. It's just grace.

Paul writing to the church at Corinth reminded them of this in 1 Corinthians 15:1–8:

Now, brothers and sisters, I want to remind you of the gospel I preached to you, which you received and on which you have taken your stand. By this gospel you are saved, if you hold firmly to the word I preached to you. Otherwise, you have believed in vain. For what I received I passed on to you as of first importance: that Christ died for our sins according to the Scriptures, that he was buried, that he was raised on the third day according to the Scriptures, and that he appeared to Cephas, and then to the Twelve. After that, he appeared to more than five hundred of the brothers and sisters at the same time, most of whom are still living, though some have fallen asleep. Then he appeared to James, then to all the apostles, and last of all he appeared to me also, as to one abnormally born.

We realize that God made a way in Jesus, and through Him, we can move from death to life. He is willing to accept us just as we are with our old paintings and frames, but He is too relentless in His great love for us to leave us where we are because He knows the masterpiece He created us to be.

If you read the Gospel accounts with this mindset, it will change the way you see the Gospel stories. Jesus is constantly moving into situations and ripping apart old paintings of sin and shame and revealing people to be who they were created to be. He would go after those most unwanted and misshapen and deformed and stained and scarred by sin and our world—the tax collectors, people of shady reputation, the blind, the lepers, the Samaritans, the shunned, the bypassed, the rejected.

And the news that God has not abandoned us was especially stunning to these people that He can actually redeem us, save us, renew us, and that life actually has meaning and purpose and significance astounded people. The reality that God's love is so deep and profound and intense and passionate and relentless that He would die for our sins left people shocked, amazed, and in awe.

It still does.

But it's all true and real and as close to you as the air you breathe.

We cannot even begin to fathom all the ways Jesus suffered for you and for me.

Jesus was betrayed and taken captive.

He was despised and rejected.

He was reviled and condemned.

He was abused and insulted.

He was falsely accused and spat upon and beaten up.

He was scourged and mocked and derided.

He was stricken and bruised and crucified.

And because of all that He went through, we can be healed.

We can move from death to life.

Listen to those words of Jesus again, from John 5:24 (NLT):

I tell you the truth, those who listen to my message and believe in God who sent me have eternal life. They will never be condemned for their sins, but they have already passed from death into life.

That's His phrase—*death to life*. And it can be trusted and relied upon.

Not only does my eternal destiny hang in the balance, but living my life to its full redemptive potential depends upon my belief and response to those life-giving words.

We can come to Jesus and allow God to create us anew in Him, to be transformed and redeemed and renewed, to allow God to rip apart the old paintings and frames of sin and shame because only He can do that. Only then we can become the masterpiece He created us to be.

Chapter 11

NEW

ew. Fresh. Original. Unique. Distinctive.
Scripture insists there is a mysterious, divine, remarkable transformation that happens for anyone who is in Christ.

Therefore, if anyone is in Christ, he is a new creation. The old has passed away; behold, the new has come. All this is from God, who through Christ reconciled us to himself and gave us the ministry of reconciliation; that is, in Christ God was reconciling the world to himself, not counting their trespasses against them, and entrusting to us the message of reconciliation. Therefore, we are ambassadors for Christ, God making his appeal through us. We implore you on behalf of Christ, be reconciled to God. For our sake he made him to be sin who knew no sin, so that in him we might become the righteousness of God.

—2 Corinthians 5:17–21 ESV

We become a new creation, created anew in Christ. Paul writes to the church in Galatia that he is in anguish to see Jesus formed in his people (Galatians 4:19). To the Romans, Paul writes, "Do not be conformed to this world, but be transformed by the renewal of your mind" (Romans 12:2). To the church in Colossae, Paul explained it in terms of taking off our old self and putting on a new self, which is an image like our Creator (Colossians 3:9–10).

The good news is that we are not the old paintings and frames of sin and shame we have been carrying all along. In Jesus, we get to understand and see and be this masterpiece God created us to be. The old, unclean paintings and frames are gone, the new, revealed masterpiece is now here.

C. S. Lewis writes in *The Weight of Glory*:

It is a serious thing to live in a society of possible gods and goddesses, to remember that the dullest and most uninteresting person you talk to may one day be a creature which, if you saw it now, you would be strongly tempted to worship, or else a horror and a corruption such as you now meet, if at all, only in a nightmare. All day long we are, in some degree, helping each other to one or other of these destinations.

The difference is Christ and His finished work on the Cross. This kind of transformation is only through the power of Christ, for we are created anew in Christ. And when we become right with our God, our Creator, our Sustainer, we start to see the greater, bigger, higher purpose we were made for, because now *He lives in us, feeding our souls with life-giving nutrients, directing our thoughts, renewing our minds, guiding our choices, and affecting every aspect of our lives.*

Paul put it this way:

I have been crucified with Christ and I no longer live, but Christ lives in me. The life I now live in the body, I live by faith in the Son of God, who loved me and gave himself for me.

—Galatians 2:20

So what is this new life, new masterpiece, and new identity? What does that mean for us today? And what are we supposed to do with it?

These are great questions. To answer these questions, let me take you to a class on cultural anthropology, something I studied in college. I quickly fell in love with the subject, and it is still an area I read about a lot.

One of the things I learned in cultural anthropology is how identity or status or value is assigned to individuals in different cultures. There are two dominant ways this is done in different cultures.

In some cultures, the dominant way people derive their identity or status or value is through ascribed status. Ascribed status is the identity, status, or value that a person is given at birth (although sometimes it can be assumed involuntarily after birth, later in life). This is not something you can earn or choose. You are assigned this status, this label, this identity. It can be either a positive or negative stereotype and is often based on family, social class, caste, race, or group into which you were born.

Therefore, people can admire, respect, and hold you in high esteem, or they can reject, disrespect, and look down upon you. Titles are seen as very important in these types of cultures. You get a serious impact on your sense of identity and your role in society and your sense of purpose because of the family you were born into and the groups you are affiliated with. Although achievements still count, your sense of identity isn't defined by what you have or have not achieved.

The other dominant way people assign status or value to a person in a culture is called achieved status. Achieved status is a sense of identity and status and value a person gains on the basis of one's merit such as achievements, assets, income, and education. A person can earn or even choose this status since it is largely an outcome of one's own efforts. Your accomplishments determine your identity and status in society. You do not necessarily get it at birth. You have to work for it and you can lose it.

Ascribed status or identity is based primarily on who you are and which group you belong to while achieved status and identity is based primarily on what you have done and can do. One is based on being, the other on doing.

From a purely cultural anthropological perspective, this is important because status and identity often come with a set of rights and duties. And there are pros and cons to both. For the purpose of this book, we will stay with the main description of these two identity shapers because they are important to understanding the individual in context.

The Bible tells us that when we are transformed by Jesus and His gospel and become a part of God's kingdom, we become a new creation. It's as if our entire sense of identity and status has gone through a change. The point is that we get this new set of ascribed status and identity that are given to us. This is not something we can earn or choose. We are assigned this status, this label, this identity. Glorious, magnificent, stunning, soul-shaping, life-giving, mind-renewing set of ascribed status and identity.

If I know Jesus as Lord and Savior,
Then I must also know that I am deeply loved,
I am cleansed and healed,
I am a friend of Jesus,
I have the grace of God,
I have the peace of God,
I have the love of God,
I have the joy of God,
I have the Spirit of God living in me,
I have been blessed with spiritual gifts,
I have been empowered to be a witness,

I am a child of the Living God,
I am a branch of the True Vine,
I am a member of Christ's body,
I am the light of the world,
I am the salt of the earth,
I am a fellow heir with Christ,
I am a new creation in Christ,
I am a citizen of the kingdom of God,
My body is the temple of the Holy Spirit,
My sins have been forgiven, from debt I am free.

And I will no longer carry the cheap, old painting that hides my true identity. I have a new painting, new status, new identity given to me by my Lord and Savior Jesus Christ who loved me so much that He died for me. And He rose again. The original Greek word used for masterpiece in Ephesians 2:10 is *poiéma*. It means something that has been made or created or crafted. There is a design and thought and purpose behind it. It has been translated as "masterpiece" but also as "workmanship," "handiwork," and "creation." It is the word from which we get the English word *poem*.

I am God's masterpiece, created to produce good works He planned for me to do long ago.

Of course, we don't just sit and enjoy this new identity we have been given. We don't just display the masterpiece; we still have work to do that He planned for us to do long ago.

Before we get to that, we need to understand something about the making of the masterpiece. *It takes time.*

I remember standing in the Louvre Museum in Paris and seeing the *Mona Lisa*. The detail, the emotion it evokes, and the admiration of art lovers and art critics alike are all unsurpassed. In terms of paintings, many scholars believe it to be the greatest masterpiece of all time. One estimate puts its value at $780 million, but since the French government is unlikely to sell it at any price, it truly is a priceless treasure. Eight million people line up each year to see it. Over the years, dust and grime have given it a coating, and throughout its colorful history there have been some attacks on the painting, which required painstaking restoration.

When you look at this masterpiece, what may not be quite as well known is that it took Leonardo da Vinci four years to finish the painting. There were long portrait sittings during which the model, believed to be the wife of an Italian cloth merchant, was entertained by musicians and jesters to make her smile. Some believe da Vinci continued to work on the painting for many years, trying to perfect it in many ways.

The same is true farther south in the Uffizi Gallery Museum in Florence. It contains some of the most famous paintings in the world. Some of the priceless treasures include the *Ognissanti Madonna* by Giotto, the *Adoration of the Magi* by Fabriano, *The Birth of Venus* by Botticelli, the *Holy Family* by Michelangelo, and many more that were stunning and breathtakingly beautiful to see. As I went on the tour, what struck me is how much time and effort went into each of these great works of art. Just across town, I also saw Michelangelo's *David*, which took the great artist three years to complete.

Creating a masterpiece takes time.

The same is true for you. It takes time—years—for the Master to work on you to reveal the masterpiece He created you to be. Sometimes He has to make a little change here or a little alteration there. The final version will not be complete this side of eternity, but it is a process that continues all through our lives. Each day, with the help of the Master Artist, we are becoming more and more like the masterpiece we were created to be, or we are becoming less and less like it.

Every day we take one small step in either one or the other direction. One easy way to identify which direction you are headed this day is to ask yourself—am I more joyful and hopeful and loving or more cynical and withdrawn and judgmental today than I was a month or a year ago?

Part of the problem is we sometimes lose our way. We may not see the whole picture. We may only see part of the plan, part of the masterpiece; we may not fully understand how God could still be at work in us.

Sometimes it may seem like God is taking a long break from His work in us, and we get confused or impatient. We may not see the work God is doing in us, and we start to doubt His promises. Or we get anxious and take matters in our own hands and move toward sin and rebellion. Or we get discouraged. How is that possible? God has given us free will—the freedom to choose. And when we do choose sin, we allow smudges and stains to once again start to cloak the masterpiece God created us to be. Dust and grime of sin start to coat it, or attacks from the enemy start to mask it, but the Master is always at work, ready to do painstaking restoration work if we turn to Him.

It happens so regularly that it's predictable. The moment I decide to do good, sin is there to trip me up. I truly delight in God's commands, but it's pretty obvious that not all of me joins in that delight. Parts of me covertly rebel, and just when I least expect it, they take charge. I've tried everything and nothing helps. I'm at the end of my rope. Is there no one who can do anything for me? Isn't that the real question? The answer, thank God, is that Jesus Christ can and does. He acted to set things right in this life of contradictions where I want to serve God with all my heart and mind, but am pulled by the influence of sin to do something totally different.

—Romans 7:21–25 *The Message*

If Jesus is Lord of our lives, we will allow Him to do the work He needs to do daily in our lives so we reflect truly and clearly and noticeably the masterpiece He created us to be.

> So all of us who have had that veil removed can see and reflect the glory of the Lord. And the Lord—who is the Spirit—makes us more and more like him as we are changed into his glorious image.
>
> —2 Corinthians 3:18 NLT

Our job is to be like clay in the Potter's hand (Isaiah 64:8). To be available and ready and willing to grow and learn and be inspired by the work of the Master in us. The one thing we cannot do, dare not do, is to remain where we are and stifle the work of the Lord in and through us. We must remain open to the new things, better things, nobler things, and healthier things He wants to do in our lives each day.

New. Fresh. Original. Unique. Distinctive.

New means leaving the old behind.

New involves moving past the cycles of remaining bound and stuck.

New entails embracing the vision the Master has for us.

New is life.

It happens and is happening for anyone who is in Christ, who understands their true identity in Christ, and who is open to the Master Artist doing His work unhindered on the canvas of our souls.

Chapter 12

TALENTS

*J*esus left us many accounts of how this masterpiece of our lives is supposed to work. Let's look at one of them. The story is found in Matthew 25:14–30 (ESV).

For it will be like a man going on a journey, who called his servants and entrusted to them his property. To one he gave five talents, to another two, to another one, to each according to his ability. Then he went away.

—vv. 14–15

The "it" Jesus is talking about is the kingdom of God. The good news is that there is a Master. He is the Owner of the talents. Scholars disagree on the actual worth of talents from our modern-day perspective, but we can safely assume that a talent was worth a large sum of money.

The Master of the Talents distributes His property among the three servants. This is their opportunity to do something with their lives. Something meaningful. Something amazing. Something extraordinary. Ordinary people don't get a chance like this.

Jesus is saying the kingdom of God is here, and everyone who calls Jesus Lord is gifted by the Master of the Talents. Not everyone is gifted the same way—each according to his ability.

Jesus is making clear that everyone is uniformly loved in the kingdom of God, but each one is uniquely gifted.

Ordinary people like you. Like me. We can enter the kingdom of God. And then the Master of the Talents gives us certain gifts. Each according to our ability. He created us. He knows exactly what He needs to give to each of us.

Jesus continues the story:

> He who had received the five talents went at once and traded with them, and he made five talents more. So also he who had the two talents made two talents more.
>
> —vv. 16–17

The text tells us that the first servant went *at once*. His reaction to this realization that He has been uniquely gifted by the Master of the Talents to invest it and use it for the kingdom was an immediate call to action. He didn't waste any time.

It happened then.
It happens now.
People come to know who Jesus is.
He is Lord. He is Savior.
Then get to taste the kingdom of God.
And then they realize everything they have
belongs to the Master of the Talents.
It is a gift.
He has entrusted his property to us.

I see people using them to bless others.
Spiritual gifts.
Material resources.
Words.

Actions.

Acts of service.

Giving their time and abilities to invest in the kingdom of God.

It's a beautiful and noble and wise thing. The investment of your God-given talents into the kingdom of God for God's purposes is the greatest investment opportunity known to humanity.

But the third servant does something different.

"But he who had received the one talent went and dug in the ground and hid his master's money" (v. 18).

Why did he do that?

He said he was afraid. Maybe he thought the Master of the Talents had a lot of money, and his one talent was too small. Maybe he thought his talent compared to others didn't matter. Maybe he thought his role was too insignificant. Maybe he was simply lazy and never got around to using his talent.

The point is, he did nothing. He didn't exercise his gifts. He didn't realize any measure of the potential he was given. He didn't use his talent. He did nothing with the opportunity and talent he was given.

There is a real danger of this happening to us on our journey to becoming the masterpiece God created us to be. We start to compare ourselves with others who seem to be more gifted and are doing great things for the kingdom of God. We start to think our role, our abilities, our time, our lives—it's too small, it's too insignificant, it doesn't matter.

The fact is, God has given you everything you need to do the good works He created you to do, to live out your purpose, to bless others, to build His kingdom. But if you keep your gaze on what others are doing, or if you keep denigrating what God has given you, you will miss this one and only chance of a lifetime.

The story does not end there. There is a sobering reminder that the Master of the Talents is coming back. And He will want an accounting of what He gave to each and every one of us.

Now after a long time the master of those servants came and settled accounts with them. And he who had received the five talents came forward, bringing five talents more, saying, "Master, you delivered to me five talents; here I have made five talents more." His master said to him, "Well done, good and faithful servant. You have been faithful over a little; I will set you over much. Enter into the joy of your master." And he also who had the two talents came forward, saying, "Master, you delivered to me two talents; here I have made two talents more." His master said to him, "Well done, good and faithful servant. You have been faithful over a little; I will set you over much. Enter into the joy of your master."

—vv. 12–23

Then the third servant comes forward, and he explains:

Master, I knew you to be a hard man, reaping where you did not sow, and gathering where you scattered no seed, so I was afraid, and I went and hid your talent in the ground. Here you have what is yours.

—vv. 24–25

The Master of the Talents is furious. He calls the third servant, "You wicked and slothful servant!" (v. 26).

Wicked and slothful. People who know Jesus, have been gifted by Him to make a difference in our world, have been created to be masterpieces, and who do nothing with their God-given gifts and talents and resources: Wicked. Slothful.

Every little gift matters to the Master of the Talents. He does not make mistakes. He knows exactly what you and I need to be the masterpiece He created us to be. When He returns He won't ask us to give an accounting of someone who received more or less talents than us. He will ask us what we did with what He gave us. However much or little that might be.

Doing nothing is an excuse that will not fly with the Master of the Talents.

Dr. Martin Luther King Jr. wrote in *Strength to Love*:

No work is insignificant. All labor that uplifts humanity has dignity and importance and should be undertaken with painstaking excellence. If a man is called to be a street sweeper, sweep streets even as a Michelangelo painted pictures, like Shakespeare wrote poetry, like Beethoven composed music, sweep streets so well that all the host of heaven and earth will have to pause and say, "Here lived a great street sweeper who swept his job well."

Do something. No matter how small. No matter how insignificant. No matter how little impact it might seem to have. That is not the point.

The point is each one of us is uniformly loved but uniquely gifted. And every little gift matters. And there is coming a day when the Master of the Talents is going to come back and ask for an account of what you and I did with the talents entrusted to us, regardless of how much or how little that may seem to any one of us.

And on that day, may His words to you and me be, "Well done, good and faithful servant."

Chapter 13

ONE CUP

In one biblical scene, we see Jesus giving some instructions to His disciples before sending them out. Toward the end of His teachings, Jesus adds a fascinating little phrase:

> And if anyone gives even a cup of cold water to one of these little ones who is my disciple, truly I tell you, that person will certainly not lose their reward.
>
> —Matthew 10:42

Why did Jesus say that? Why did Jesus say "a cup of cold water"? Why not two cups of cold water? Why not ten? Why not hundred? Why not thousand? Why not say, "He who digs a well and an entire village can have clean drinking water?" Why not say, "He who finds a way to provide clean drinking water to everyone who doesn't have access to it" (approximately 650 million people in the world)?

Why not highlight that? Why just one cup? Fascinating, isn't it? Jesus says "a cup." And Jesus says that's great!

In 2016, billionaire Phil Knight, cofounder and chairman of Nike, gave $400 million to Stanford University, the largest donation in the school's history—it made front-page news.

A few years ago Joan Kroc, the widow of McDonald's restaurant magnate Ray Kroc, left $1.5 billion to Salvation Army. That made front-page news. We often hear of millions given to this cause or that cause, and it's all good and proper and wonderful.

And Jesus says, "Wait, wait, wait. Did you see that widow who came to church last weekend? Her husband died and left her with nothing. She has given her heart and life to me. I know her. She is barely making it on Social Security. Then the pastor spoke about missions and the need for orphans and widows in Central America, and she put in five dollars."

That became front-page news in the kingdom of God. That's what is trending on Twitter in heaven!

Every act of generosity matters,
When it is done with a heart surrendered to Jesus.
Every act of patience,
Every act of self-sacrificing love,
Every act of joyful service,
Every word of comfort or compassion or reassurance,
Every single time you exercise self-control and say no to sin,
Every smile offered by the church parking lot team,
Every warm welcome extended in the lobby
before the church service,
Every hug to an orphan, every dollar that goes
to sponsor a child in a third-world country,
Every outreach to a veteran or a senior or the homeless,
Every visit to a hospital,
Every conversation with a couple whose marriage is in crisis,
Every attempt to build community,
Every soul-shaping word spoken into a teenager,
Every song, every sermon, every story, every prayer,
Every act of grace,
Every cup of water—it matters.

We live in a world where big impact is celebrated, a world where viral YouTube videos and memes grab our attention, a world where it feels good to have our own few minutes in the limelight. Don't wait for that. Don't delay using this time, this day, this very moment. Don't postpone using your gifts, your passion, and your talents. Do what He's calling you to do today. Be generous, extend love to a little one, plant hope where you see despair, infuse joy where you see pain, ignite a light where you see darkness, or speak life into a jaded soul.

One cup. Little things. Small acts. You never know where the ripple will stop. They all count.

God asks Moses, "What is in your hand?" (Exodus 4:2). It's just a staff. God can use that. Samson had a jawbone (Judges 15). David had five smooth stones (1 Samuel 17:40). The widow of Zarephath had a handful of flour and a little oil (1 Kings 17). The little boy had five small loaves and two small fish (John 6).

One Sunday, after I had preached, one of our long-time members came to talk to me. She is a remarkable woman with many talents and gifts. After she had children, she decided to stay at home and be a full-time homemaker. Her kids are grown now, and she had been out of the corporate world for many years. She told me how with all her education and experience in the corporate field, she felt she was not making an impact or difference for Jesus as she ought. So we prayed that God would remove the scales from her eyes so she could see all the ways she makes a difference and all the opportunities He brings her way every day. I told her to write all the *little* ways God was going to use her that week.

She sent me an email a week later and told me how after she had left church, she had a peace about her. She said how the words *little things* hit her and how she was viewing things differently.

She sent me a list of things that happened that week for her. A friend showed up at her house unannounced, and they were able to reconnect in ways that made them both realize how they can make a difference in their community. She was at a doctor's office and had a book and then felt prompted to give the book to the lab technician. She said the lab technician was thrilled to get that particular book because of what she was going through at that moment in her life.

She wrote how she was walking her dog and met someone in her neighborhood, and they started talking. The neighbor confided in her that she was going through a devastating divorce, and she was able to minister and pray with her. She arrived at her book club and struck up a conversation with a woman who needed encouragement. She attended a community event and made two new friends. She met another woman who has a ministry to high school students about making smart choices and invited her to join in. She realized her gifts were a perfect match for this volunteer opportunity and that it would make such a difference in the lives of teenagers.

Then she wrote, "God is working, and I am realizing how the littlest things can make a difference."

That's how things work in the kingdom of God. Jesus said, in Matthew 13:31–32:

> The kingdom of heaven is like a mustard seed, which a man took and planted in his field. Though it is the smallest of all seeds, yet when it grows, it is the largest of garden plants and becomes a tree, so that the birds come and perch in its branches.

The littlest things matter in the kingdom of God. And you never know how they may impact the life of someone else and the ripple effect you unleash when you partner with God to do the little things He is calling you to do today. The principal of my high school used to say, "Anyone can count the number of seeds in an apple. Only God can count the number of apples in one seed."

You just never know what can happen to a mustard seed when it is planted. You can't immediately see how it is going to grow and how its growth and life will bless others.

It's the heart.
It's the faith.
It's the trust.
It's the redemptive and transformative work
that is going on in us and through us as we take that step
and offer what is in our hands to God.

Do not despise these small beginnings, for the LORD rejoices to see the work begin.
—Zechariah 4:10 NLT

When Rachel Cinader found out that in some parts of the world there are little girls who have no dresses, she decided something needed to be done. A girl without a dress is more prone to abuse; one dress for a little girl can drastically reduce her chances of being abused.

This was an illuminating moment for her soul—the spark, the defining moment, the unrelenting impulse in her heart—that refused to go away. She just couldn't let it go. After praying and wrestling with it, she decided to *use a pillowcase* to make a dress for a little girl, with holes for the neck and arms and belt to tie it at the waist. She thought, *I can do that.*

She started a tiny ministry and named it Dress a Girl Around the World because she was convicted that every little girl on earth deserves at least one dress. It's a way to show girls around the world that they are precious to God.

She started sewing these simple, cotton dresses and very soon, other dressmakers joined her. Today, she has ambassadors across the United States who make these dresses for little girls who would otherwise have none. To date, Rachel Cinader's *little* ministry has shipped well more than 300,000 dresses to 81 countries. Hundreds of thousands of little girls now have at least one dress to wear.

One story.

One spark.

One life.

One tiny mustard seed.

One cup.

One pillowcase.

Anyone can do something. Jesus said in Luke 16:10, "Whoever can be trusted with very little can also be trusted with much, and whoever is dishonest with very little will also be dishonest with much."

God's goal is to grow us in our character, in our love for Him and others, and become more and more like the masterpiece He created us to be. And to do that He often gives us this one day, this one moment, this one conversation, this one person, this one cup in front of us, the little things to see how we handle that before He can trust us with more.

When we learn to handle the holiness and the significance and the responsibility in the opportunity of the one cup, we can graduate to the ministry of two cups.

Chapter 14

SILENCE

The quietest wild place in the United States of America is located at 47°51'57.5" N, 123°52'13.3" W. This is also known as the quietest square inch of land in America. It is not quiet because of the total lack of sound, since it is located inside Washington State Olympic National Park. The quiet designation comes from the lack of noise of human origin, that is, for the time being.

This spot is marked by a red pebble and so named by Emmy Award–winning acoustic ecologist Gordon Hempton. He has been recording natural sounds for more than 35 years. In the article, "Welcome to the Quietest Square Inch in the US" by *Outside* magazine, Hempton says, "Unless something is done, we'll see the complete extinction of quiet in the US in our lifetime."

There is a furious urgency for calm in our souls.

Why is quiet and silence so hard for us in the first world? Noise is everywhere around us. From the time we wake up to the sound of an alarm clock to the time we dose off to the glow of the television. It is our constant companion—the buzz, the chatter, the clamor.

Our days are filled with
Chores,
Driving,
Shopping,
Working,

Texting,

Email,

Internet,

Smartphones,

Tablets,

Facebook,

Twitter,

Video games,

YouTube,

Sports,

Music,

And television.

The prophet Isaiah wrote:

This is what the Sovereign LORD, the Holy One of Israel, says: "In repentance and rest is your salvation, in quietness and trust is your strength, but you would have none of it."

—Isaiah 30:15

We would have none of it because we are so surrounded by noise and status updates and push notifications. These things force us to slice and scatter our attention into multiple things. We have options. We have channels. We have apps. Our time and thoughts and days leak out in hundreds of small drains, and it takes us away from the greater things.

This is nothing new. In the Gospel of Luke, we find the story of Mary and Martha (Luke 10:38–42). Martha often gets typecast in this story, but the text starts by telling us that she opened her home to Jesus. She knows Jesus. She opened her home to Him. She was making preparations, likely for her guests.

Mary, her sister, sits at the feet of Jesus, listening, learning, and soaking in the words of Jesus. Martha is upset by this. What is interesting is how Luke writes the story. His choice of word for Martha is very telling. He says she is "distracted" (v. 40). Jesus gently reminds her that Mary had chosen the one thing that is needed. What is this one thing? It's not that she would sit at the feet of Jesus for the rest of her life. It's that she stayed and lived and spent her days in awareness of the presence of Christ.

Jesus knows how our distractions can keep us from living a life centered on Him. The constant connection we have with the world via the Internet forces us to pay attention to a hundred little things ahead of the "one thing" that is needed for us each day—to start and live this day, which the Lord has made, in recognition of His presence in it.

It is not unusual to see the digital distractions jostling and poking and pushing its way into family time, during meals, finding its way into the tiniest slivers of time of our days.

Charles Spurgeon exhorts us in his book *Lectures to My Students*:

Think not to be a messenger of grace to others till you have seen the God of grace for yourselves, and had the word from his mouth. Time spent in quiet prostration of soul before the Lord is most invigorating. David "sat before the Lord"; it is a great thing to hold these sacred sittings; the mind being receptive, like an open flower drinking in the sunbeams, or the sensitive photographic plate accepting the image before it.

In an article titled, "Finding God in the Depths of Silence" from *Sojourners* magazine, author Richard Rohr writes:

More than ever, because of iPads, cell phones, billboards, TVs, and iPods, we are a toxically overstimulated people. Only time will tell the deep effects of this on emotional maturity, relationship, communication, conversation, and religion itself. Silence now seems like a luxury. . . . Without it, most liturgies, Bible studies, devotions, "holy" practices, sermons, and religious conversations might be good and fine, but they will never be truly great or life-changing—for ourselves or for others. They can only represent the surface; God is always found at the depths, even the depths of our sin and brokenness. And in the depths, it is silent.

Earlier on he wrote the line that made me pause and think, "The ego gets what it wants with words. The soul finds what it needs in silence."

On the other hand, when we are overwhelmed and in turmoil, the words of David exhort us in Psalm 4:4 (NLT), "Think about it overnight and remain silent." And again in Psalm 37:7 (NLT), "Be still in the presence of the LORD, and wait patiently for him to act." And again in Psalm 62:1–2 (NLT), "I wait quietly before God, for my victory comes from him. He alone is my rock and my salvation, my fortress where I will never be shaken."

God works in the midst of our daily work, daily living, and daily challenges. However, if we remain a soul fragmented and distracted by the many diversions, interruptions, and amusements, we will miss some of God's most significant whispers.

Whispers that gently decalcify the hardened old paintings of our lives, whispers that call us to a higher purpose, whispers that softly nudge us in the way we should go, whispers that give us a divine mandate, whispers that warn us, admonish us, teach us, shape us, and mold us into the masterpieces we were created to be.

In those moments when we sit at the feet of Jesus, we listen and learn and soak in and then take the instructions and whispers and promptings and words of Jesus into our relationships, our work, our commute, and our families. It can impact every aspect of our lives. It keeps us grounded. This "one thing" helps us see all other things in perspective.

To experience this we need to know and listen to the voice of our Lord.

> **Knowing Christ through times away in solitude and silence will "let our joy be full" (see John 16:24). It will bring over us a pervasive sense of well-being, no matter what is happening around us. Hurry and the loneliness of leadership will be eliminated. We can allow the peace of God to sink deeply into our lives and extend through our relationships to others (see Matthew 10:12-13). . . . Solitude and silence are absolutely basic in our responsibility to soul care. But they also open before us the whole area of disciplines for the spiritual life. It is vital for us to keep before us that there are tried and true ways we can pursue toward abundant life in Christ. . . . We can and must incorporate these into our lives as completely reliable ways of personal soul care. There is no substitute for this.**
>
> —Professor Dallas Willard, *The Great Omission*

My sheep listen to my voice; I know them, and they follow me. I give them eternal life, and they shall never perish; no one will snatch them out of my hand. My Father, who has given them to me, is greater than all; no one can snatch them out of my Father's hand.

—John 10:27–29

We can hear His voice *if we take the time to listen*. Listening can be hard in our noisy world. But without listening, we cannot know. Without knowing, we cannot obey and follow and do the things Jesus wants to do in our lives to make us the masterpiece He created us to be.

"In solitude," Henri Nouwen writes, "I get rid of my scaffolding: no friends to talk with, no telephone calls to make, no meetings to attend, no music to entertain, no books to distract, just me—naked, vulnerable, weak, sinful, deprived, broken."

There is freedom there, there is light there, there is the slow and deliberative work to reveal the you you were created to be.

If silence is new to you, I suggest Richard Foster's classic book, *Celebration of Discipline*. You will find a host of great ideas and thoughts about silence and solitude. Foster suggests we take even tiny snatches of time we have at our disposal every day and make them times of inner quiet, in essence symbolically sit at the feet of Jesus—those early morning moments, a morning cup of coffee, when stuck traffic. We can go a step further and create space in our home (such as a quiet corner) or in our community (such as a park bench).

Maybe you can simply say a prayer in these moments, "Lord, help me, guide me, teach me, mold me, and grow me."

Do it not as a law, but as an experiment, as an opportunity to allow God to speak into you, to dismantle the shell of old paintings and to reveal to you the masterpiece you were created to be, to show you the places in your life where grime and dust of sin and habits start to shroud the masterpiece. To be able to hear all of that without the distractions of our times—that is the goal.

In *Life Together*, Dietrich Bonhoeffer wrote:

We are silent at the beginning of the day because God should have the first word, and we are silent before going to sleep

because the last word also belongs to God . . . Silence is nothing else but waiting for God's Word and coming from God's Word with a blessing. But everybody knows that this is something that needs to be practiced and learned, in these days when talkativeness prevails. Real silence, real stillness, really holding one's tongue comes only as the sober consequence of spiritual stillness.

For God to dismantle our old selves and reveal to us our new selves, we need to be able to listen to Him. God's voice comes to us in many ways—His Word, prayer, sermons, community, and friends, being involved in kingdom work are some ways God speaks to us. But God also speaks to us through the gentle whispers, through the silence, through the stillness. To practice this, it is important to note what this is not.

Silence is not a legalistic requirement.

Silence is also not a way to become spiritually superior to others.

Dallas Willard reminds us in *The Spirit of the Disciplines* that, "We can only survive solitude if we cling to Christ."

Silence is not loneliness.

Loneliness is the absence of community, of relational connections we were made for.

Silence is the absence of distractions often for a short intentional period of time.

Silence is fasting from noise.

The writer of Ecclesiastes reminds us that there is "a time to be silent and a time to speak" (Ecclesiastes 3:7). Jesus did this. He spent a significant amount of time alone, praying and fasting, before the start of His public ministry (Matthew 4). He spent an entire night alone praying before choosing His disciples (Luke 6:12–16). He would often withdraw to lonely places (Luke 5:16).

You see this rhythm in the life of Christ—busy schedules and snatches of time alone or with close community.

   Be still, and know that I am God.
                                          —Psalm 46:10

Quietness and solitude are among the important ways God works in our lives and reveals to us the masterpieces He has created us to be.

If you have never done this, or it's been a while, try this as a first step: find a quiet space in your life for about 30 minutes. Slowly read Psalms 138 and 139, and reflect on them without any distractions.

Chapter 15

REMAINS

Masterpiece.

Work of art.

Magnum opus.

God's handiwork.

Me?

Me? With my issues and problems and scars?

Me? Whose life is a mess?

**Me? Someone who feels weary and withdrawn
and worn out?**

Me? Broken me? Battered me? Bruised me?

Me?

his talk of a masterpiece may seem like a joke to you, if you are someone going through a tough time, a mess of circumstances, or the blue skies of your life have turned gray and even thicker, darker storm clouds have ominously appeared in the horizon.

Or you thought life was going to turn out a certain way, and are now resigned to a new normal of reduced expectations from the world, from yourself, from God.

Or divorce, betrayal, rejection, cheating, abuse, unemployment, bankruptcy, loss, a lab report has left you reeling.

Masterpiece?

Me?

Really?

An angel appears to a man who is hiding in a pit in the ground, threshing wheat. The angel looks at him and says a most remarkable thing, "The LORD is with you, mighty warrior" (Judges 6:12).

Huh?

The economy had tanked, unemployment was up, people were having a hard time making ends meet, and Israel was a plundered nation. This has been going on for seven years. The enemy, the Midianites and Amalekites among others, would come suddenly from time to time and kill their cattle and destroy their crops. They would come like a dreaded swarm of locusts.

And the angel of the Lord comes to a most unlikely person, and he knows it.

Me?

With my issues and problems and scars?

Whose life is a mess?

Someone who feels weary and withdrawn and worn out?

Broken me? Battered me? Bruised me?

Me?

Gideon responds to God's call this way: "Pardon me, my lord . . . but how can I save Israel? My clan is the weakest in Manasseh, and I am the least in my family (v. 15).

Weakest.

Least.

Insignificant.

No, no, no, Gideon. Those are all old paintings and frames. Inside of you there is the masterpiece of a mighty hero waiting to come out. The one you were created to be in the first place. Trust me.

But Mr. Angel, you do not understand, Gideon argues. *We are a forgotten people, we are the weak, the ignored, the least.*

My choices.

My habits.

My past.

My life.

My failures.

My problems.

My circumstances.

My sickness.

My loss.

They have left me weak and weary and discouraged.

What can God do with the relics of my life?

I have to be content with where I am, who I am, what I have become—make the best of the mess.

He can't make music out of a broken, old, beat-up instrument.

Or can He?

In more than two decades of my ministry in the United States and abroad, I have seen and experienced certain things, especially within the community of Christ. I have had the joy of sharing happy moments such as marriages and baby dedications, and I have been both humbled and honored to be in that sacred space when someone is close to death. I have seen people go through devastating news and face it with uncommon courage. I have seen someone come out of heartbreaking betrayal and slowly and steadfastly rebuild his or her life. I have seen people bear unbelievable loss and face it with a deep abiding sense of fortitude. I have seen ordinary people face overwhelming setbacks with extraordinary faith.

I have seen those bound by chains of addictions find freedom. I have seen couples whose marriages were on the brink find reconciliation and renew their vows. I have seen people healed, I have seen people climb out from the pit of despair and failure and make something beautiful out of their lives.

We all carry scars of living in a broken world. Sin impacts us all. We all fall short. And sometimes the answers don't come easy. Life is a mixed bag of opportunities and challenges, setbacks and successes. I do not claim to understand the why behind human pain and suffering. Much has been written about that subject. What I do know is this—when someone decides to turn what remains in the hands of God, it doesn't fix everything the way we want it or make everything OK, but something special and radiant and remarkable often comes out of it.

Novelist Anne Lamott wrote an article titled "Becoming the Person You Were Meant to Be" for *O: The Oprah Magazine* in which she says:

> **Here's how I became myself: mess, failure, mistakes, disappointments . . . limbo, indecision, setbacks, addiction, public embarrassment, and endless conversations with my best women friends; the loss of people without whom I could not live, the loss of pets that left me reeling, dizzying betrayals but much greater loyalty, and overall, choosing as my motto William Blake's line that we are here to learn to endure the beams of love. . . . Wherever the great dilemma exists is where the great growth is, too. . . . [And at the center] is you. Fabulous, hilarious, darling, screwed-up you. Beloved of God and of your truest deepest self, the self that is revealed when tears wash off the makeup and grime. The self that is revealed when dealing with your anger blows through all the calcification in your soul's pipes.**

Fact is, we can bring all our mess, our loss, our past, what remains of our lives to God, and He can still use it to make something beautiful. It doesn't matter how bad your life, your circumstances, and your past have been. What matters is whether you are open to God to reveal the masterpiece in the midst of pain and loss and suffering. Are you willing to let Him work with what remains in your life?

Are you willing to trust Him with it?

It happened with Gideon one day—a scared, weak, lonely man in an oppressed country.

It happened to Abraham, an old man with the promise of a son.

It happened to Moses, a shepherd who wasn't the best speaker.

It happened to Rahab, it happened to David, it happened to Elijah, it happened to Jonah, it happened to Matthew and James and John and Zacchaeus and Mary Magdalene and Paul.

Can God make music out of a broken, old, beat-up instrument? Yes. He. Can.

If you trust Him,
No matter how hopeless the situation of life seems,
No matter what the locusts have taken,
No matter what remains of your life,
He can still continue to work on you
and redeem and restore and reveal
the masterpiece you were created to be.

And I am sure of this, that He who began a good work in you will bring it to completion at the day of Jesus Christ.

—Philippians 1:6 ESV

Chapter 16

TODAY

*T*oday is God's brand new creation.

The Apostle Paul reminds us, "Rejoice always, pray continually, give thanks in all circumstances; for this is God's will for you in Christ Jesus" (Philippians 5:16–18).

The prophet Jeremiah writes, "The steadfast love of the Lord never ceases; his mercies never come to an end; they are new every morning; great is your faithfulness" (Lamentations 3:22–23 ESV).

God made today, this hour, this very moment.

**It may not feel that way when you get up in the morning
to an alarm clock,
Look at yourself in the mirror in the bathroom,
Stress about getting the kids to school in time,
Get ready for work,
Sit still in traffic,
Labor on what seems like a meaningless project at work,
Sit through a boring meeting,
Listen to your boss drone on about something
even he or she is not excited about,
Get back home and rush to get dinner on the table
or simply stop by McDonald's,
Clean the kitchen,
Get the kids ready for bed,**

Stress about high credit-card debt
as you decide which bills to pay,
Drop in front of television half-comatose,
Drift off to sleep.

The days drag and the years whiz past.
Maybe that's you.
Maybe not.
But most days can feel quite ordinary
and unremarkable and boring,
And we cannot fathom
a whole lot of things we can rejoice about.

And yet, God's work is happening in the here and now. Right in the middle of getting up in the morning, in the traffic, in the workplace, at dinner, doing the dishes, paying the bills, when you are in crisis—right there, right then, God is at work. Stuff is happening in the unseen realms to gear us and make us and mold us into the masterpieces we were created to be. *God's presence is as close to you as a conscious thought, a heartfelt prayer, a moment's sense of gratitude, and a quiet and earnest call for help.*

God is present, and His work is happening right here right now. We can choose to live in ignorance of it. And by doing that, we cut off the power of His life-giving, mind-renewing, soul-shaping, masterpiece-making work in our lives.

Nicholas Herman knew this only too well. Nicholas was born to peasant parents in France around 1611. While still a young man, he joined the army, perhaps forced into it so that he could get enough food to eat and a small income. While in the army, Nicholas had a profound spiritual experience. One winter, he happened to look at a tree stripped of all its leaves. As he looked on, he was overcome with the sense that he was like that tree, seemingly devoid of life.

But then the realization came to him that winter will end and spring will come and with it bring new life. That bare tree, Nicholas wrote, "flashed in upon my soul the fact of God."

A few years later, he would join a monastery in Paris and become known as Brother Lawrence. His job was that of a cook. He found unusual joy in the everyday tedious and dreary tasks of cooking and cleaning. He would dispense his wisdom about how every day, every moment, every task, could be enjoyed and done for the glory of God.

Consider these words of Brother Lawrence:

Nor is it needful that we should have great things to do . . . We can do little things for God. I turn the cake that is frying on the pan for the love of Him. When that is done, if there is nothing else to call me, I prostrate myself in worship before Him, who has given me grace to work; afterwards, I rise happier than a king. It is enough for me to pick up but a straw from the ground for the love of God.

Brother Lawrence cooked meals, cleaned the kitchen, ran errands, and did countless other orders of his superiors as if he were completing the greatest tasks in the world. He knew what it meant to live the words of the Apostle Paul in Colossians 3:23–24:

Whatever you do, work at it with all your heart, as working for the Lord, not for human masters, since you know that you will receive an inheritance from the Lord as a reward. It is the Lord Christ you are serving.

Eugene Peterson puts it this way in his translation of the Bible, *The Message*:

In time of crisis everything, absolutely every-thing, is important and significant. Life itself is on the line. No word is casual, no action marginal. And almost always, God and our relationship with God is on the front page. But during the humdrum times, when things are, as we tend to say, "normal," our interest in God is crowded to the margins of our lives and we become preoccupied with ourselves. . . . treating the worship of God as a mere hobby or diversion, managing our personal affairs . . . for our own convenience and disregarding what God has to say about them, going about our usual activities *as if God were not involved in such dailiness.* (author's emphasis)

Brother Lawrence never gained fame or fortune during his lifetime. His sayings and words were put together and published after his death. That resulting book became one of the more enduring spiritual classics of all time. Since its publication, millions of copies have continued to be produced.

Part of the process of becoming a masterpiece is recognizing God's presence and His work and His mission this day, this hour, this moment. Brother Lawrence made every moment of his life a conscious moment of being with the God who created him to be a masterpiece this day, this moment, in this kitchen, in this monastery, in the midst of the mundane, the ordinary, the tedious, and the dreary, God is here and at work. He lived in intentional recognition of it.

Frederick Buechner distilled his life's teachings in his second memoir, *Now and Then*, this way:

If I were called upon to state in a few words the essence of everything I was trying to say both as a novelist and as a

preacher, it would be something like this: Listen to your life. See it for the fathomless mystery that it is. In the boredom and pain of it no less than in the excitement and gladness: touch, taste, smell your way to the holy and hidden heart of it, because in the last analysis all moments are key moments, and life itself is grace.

Our problem is that not all moments appear to be key moments, and life does not feel like grace. But if today is all we've got, wouldn't it be better to walk in it with a sense of gratitude and anticipation and in recognition of God's presence and His work in and around us? What would happen to you and to me if we did wash dishes for the love of God? Or attended that meeting for the love of God? Or spoke life into a stressed-out co-worker no one wants to be friends with? Or engaged with our kids for 30 minutes without having anything "more important" pull us away? Or sat in the car stuck in traffic praising and rejoicing? Insane, isn't it?

The truth is, we all struggle with this—the pull between the kingdom of God and the kingdom of Earth. One reveals a whole new me that God is making me to be, and the other clouds the masterpiece with the grime of jadedness and cynicism and boredom.

When my oldest, Elizabeth, was in second grade, she had a field trip to an orchard near where we live for a fall festival. They invited one parent to go with each child. Usually it's my wife, but I decided to go on this one. The whole place was teeming with students and teachers and parents. They had all kinds of games and hayrides and pumpkin patches.

I was walking with the kids and taking everything in when we stumbled upon a huge stack of hay.

Elizabeth looked at me and said, "Dad, throw me on that big pile of hay?"

So I picked her up, swung her over my shoulder, and threw her on that pile of hay. She gave out these really loud squeals of laughter.

"Do it again, Dad!"

So we did it again. And again. And again. I started feeling tired and wanted to stop.

But then her two friends, Hannah and Michelle, quickly joined in, and I threw them on that pile of hay as well. They were laughing and screaming with joy. Other kids and parents lined up. I guess they thought I worked at that place and was part of the attractions!

"Do it again!"

In his book *Orthodoxy*, G. K. Chesterton writes:

A child kicks his legs rhythmically through excess, not absence, of life. Because children have abounding vitality, because they are in spirit fierce and free, therefore they want things repeated and unchanged. They always say, "Do it again"; and the grown-up person does it again until he is nearly dead. For grown-up people are not strong enough to exult in monotony. But perhaps God is strong enough to exult in monotony. It is possible that God says every morning, "Do it again" to the sun; and every evening, "Do it again" to the moon. It may not be automatic necessity that makes all daisies alike; it may be that God makes every daisy separately, but has never got tired of making them. It may be that He has the eternal appetite of infancy; for we have sinned and grown old, and our Father is younger than we.

I understood what Chesterton meant that day at the orchard throwing my little girl and her friends on a pile of hay.

And right in the middle of it all, with a small crowd gathered there, Elizabeth suddenly stopped and yelled out a phrase I will never forget in my life. And the words came out very loud and clear and the words came from the depths of her belly. I mean, she joyously screamed these words—

"Isn't my dad awesome?"

These words had a magical effect on me. I felt my heart surge with joy. Just a moment ago, I had made up my mind that I wasn't going to throw them on the pile of hay anymore because I was feeling tired. All of a sudden, I wasn't feeling tired anymore.

So I threw them on that pile of hay a third, fourth, and fifth time. I did that for 30 minutes straight until one of the orchard employees came and stopped me for "liability" reasons.

Sometimes we forget that God is also a Father. He is not some extraterrestrial being, a cosmic Santa Claus, or some abstract artificial intelligence. And this God desires a relationship with us. He wants us to experience the same joy He has, the kind we sometimes see in kids.

What if tomorrow you and I and all of God's children got up, saw the sun, and said, "Isn't my Dad awesome? Do it again, Dad!"

What if we ate our breakfast and reflected on the blessing of our daily bread and said, "Isn't my Dad awesome? Do it again, Dad!"

What if on the way to work, we reflected on the fact we have a job, that God has provided work for us to do, or that somehow He has and will provide, and we said, "Isn't my Dad awesome? Do it again, Dad!"

What if at work when we faced challenges and choices and meetings and projects, we cast our worries on Him and recognized that, "Isn't my Dad awesome? Do it again, Dad!"

What if those around you saw you smiling and joyful as you go about daily chores, and they learn you are doing that and can only do that because, you know, "Isn't my Dad awesome? Do it again, Dad!"

What if tomorrow you were facing some of the most painful circumstances of your life, and you said to yourself, "I will never waste a crisis," and, "I will use this to strengthen my faith in God." And what if you said, "I will follow God with reckless abandon" because: "Isn't my Dad awesome? Do it again, Dad!"

What if tomorrow, throughout the day, you asked God to fill you with His love, His blessings, His mercy, and His joy? He will, and all you say in response is, "Isn't my Dad awesome? Do it again, Dad!"

If you and I lived that way, what would that do to the heart of God? More importantly, what would that do to our hearts and minds and souls?

It would dramatically reveal the masterpiece God created us to be as we allow the joy of our Lord to wash away the grime of cynicism and discouragement and jadedness.

What if tomorrow you and I lived with the maxim of "It is enough for me to pick up but a straw from the ground for the love of God"?

We would live out Paul's words:

Rejoice, take delight, be joyful,
Pray, pray with joy, pray with hope, pray with faith,
Give thanks, because your Dad is awesome!

That's God's will for us on how we should live today. It's how the dust and grime get swabbed away. It's how a little more of the masterpiece gets revealed each day.

Part Four
GALLERY

There is nothing like the local church when it's working right. Its beauty is indescribable. Its power is breathtaking. Its potential is unlimited. It comforts the grieving and heals the broken in the context of community. It builds bridges to seekers and offers truth to the confused. It provides resources to those in need and opens its arms to the forgotten, the downtrodden, the disillusioned. It breaks the chains of addictions, frees the oppressed, and offers hope to the marginalized in this world. Whatever the capacity for human suffering, the church has a greater capacity for healing and wholeness. . . . The potential of the local church is almost more than I can grasp.

— Bill Hybels, *Courageous Leadership*

Chapter 17

MOSAIC

I was walking down a long corridor at terminal 5 of Heathrow Airport in London when I noticed a giant picture of a British Airways aircraft. From a distance, the picture looked regal and stunning and eye-catching. But as I walked closer, I started noticing that this massive image of a British Airways plane seemed pixelated. That seemed odd. I kept moving toward it, and when I came closer, I understood why.

This giant photo was actually not a photo of an airplane at all. It was a photo mosaic. In other words, it was made up of thousands of little photos. The thousands of tiny photos covered every country the airline serves. When I came within a few feet of it, I could see they took pictures of people from around the world in different settings and put it together in such a way that from a distance, the larger image looked like a British Airways aircraft. It was a picture made up of many smaller pictures.

Yes, God created you anew in Christ to be a masterpiece, but let's go back and look at a crucial pronoun in Ephesians 2:10 (NLT), "For we are God's masterpiece."

The key word here is "we"—every pronoun in Ephesians 2 is in the plural.

We.

Not just me.

There is no way we can be a masterpiece in isolation.

In other words, the church is the ultimate masterpiece of God!

The church.

The bride of Christ.

The body of Christ.

The people of God.

The community of Jesus.

Paul insists we are God's masterpiece. His work of art. There is a design and thought and purpose behind it all. Each of us is like that little picture inside of the big picture. The church is the giant photo mosaic of a masterpiece made of millions of little masterpieces.

Another way of looking at it is to say that the church is like a gallery of masterpieces. As I mentioned earlier, one of the world's best-known galleries of masterpieces is the Uffizi Gallery Museum in Florence, Italy. It houses masterpieces of art luminaries like Giotto, Fabriano, Michelangelo, Raphael, da Vinci, Rembrandt, Botticelli, and many others. People line up for hours during high season to get in. The beauty and the purpose and the genius and the brilliance of these gifted artists are reflected in their work.

Paul says we are to be like that. *A gathering, a community, a collection of masterpieces created by the Master Artist to reflect the beauty and the purpose and the genius and the brilliance of our Maker, our Creator, our Lord.*

That is why when people say they love Jesus but not the church, they miss the whole point of being a masterpiece of God. It can never be achieved in isolation. It can only and always be achieved in community.

The church was meant to be the gathering and display and release of the *poiema* of God, to reflect the beauty and the purpose and the genius and the brilliance of its Master Artist.

And Paul lays out that the role of this masterpiece, the community of Jesus, is to do the good works, individually and collectively, that God has planned, prepared, and ordained for us to do a long time ago.

The works here are not a way to earn grace.

We can't earn God's grace.

We don't merit it, and we don't deserve it.

That's why it's grace.

So works are the fruit of this grace. In fact, Jesus "gave Himself for us to redeem us from from all wickedness and to purify for himself a people that are his very own, eager to do what is good" (Titus 2:14).

One of our joys is to seek, discover, and fulfill that plan in tandem with the community of Christ. This has been the plan of God for you from even before the day you were born! To say it another way, the day you start the journey with Jesus is not the end, but the beginning of this plan. When you are in Christ, you become a new creation (2 Corinthians 5:17). But God continues to work in you so that you can be conformed to the image of Christ (Romans 8:29).

Back to the works Paul is writing about. He weaves two characteristics to these works. The first thing to note is that these are to be good works (as opposed to evil or wicked works). Jesus said as much in Matthew 5:16 that we are to let our light shine before the world so that they may see our good works and glorify our Father in heaven. Paul exhorts the community of Christ in Corinth to excel, flourish, and abound in every good work. (2 Corinthians 9:8). He tells Timothy to be equipped and prepared for every good work (2 Timothy 3:17). To the church at Colossae, Paul says they should produce, bear, and bring forth every good work (Colossians 1:10). This is what happens to a person and a community of Christ that is in the grip of grace; he and it understand the idea of how we are created individually and collectively to be a masterpiece. These good works are a result of God at work in and through us.

The second thing to see is that the good works have been prepared for us. He ordained these works a long time ago. Elsewhere, Paul says, God's desire is to "make the riches of his glory shine even brighter on those to whom he shows mercy, who were prepared in advance for glory" (Romans 9:23 NLT).

We are not just another name or number or face. Without our pictures, the great mosaic of the church will be full of holes and incomplete.

Therefore, the role of the church is to not only help us discover our true identity, but also our true mission. Like the disciples, this will mean following a Lord who calls us to a risky, sometimes demanding, often countercultural way of life.

A way of life that is adventurous, hopeful, and that frequently compels us to deny ourselves.

A way of life that follows a different set of rules when it comes to friendship and marriage and generosity and integrity and work ethics and dealing with the poor and the orphans and the widows.

A way of life to be lived in a messy, wonderful, eclectic, flourishing community with people from all backgrounds and races and genders and statuses and ethnicities.

I experienced this in a fresh way recently. I had almost completed the sermon I was going to preach the following weekend when I came across an article about developing a great speech. Knowing what I do for a living, I read it—the key point was to always know your audience. Analyze your audience. Find something that is common to the people in your audience.

Always looking for ways to get better at what I do, I thought, *If my church is my audience, then I should analyze my audience.*

I thought about the 1,300 or so people that gather each Sunday. I thought of faces and names and families.

So I started writing about who will be there this weekend. And here's what I came up with:

The happy, the sad,
The hurting, the joyful,
The recently divorced and the recently married,
The senior citizen and the brand-new teenager,

The American and the immigrant,

The Republican and the Democrat,

The rich and the poor,

The black and the white,

The CEOs and the unemployed,

The cops and the ex-felons,

The Jew and the Gentile,

The heartbroken, the happy, the grieving, the joyful,

The sinner and the saint,

The grace-seeker and the peace-seeker,

The lonely and the lost,

The redeemed and the heavily burdened,

The millennial and the baby boomer.

We are all here. In this place called the church. The article wasn't helpful to me because the source of our inspiration and mission and even the sermon is the Living Word of God. It is "alive and active. Sharper than any double-edged sword, it penetrates even to dividing soul and spirit, joints and marrow; it judges the thoughts and attitudes of the heart (Hebrews 4:12). And when we gather under the authority of Jesus as revealed in the Word, there isn't any one narrow definition of this community, this body, this bride of Christ.

You will not find such a community anywhere else.

You will not find it among the workforce of Apple.

You will not find it in the personnel ranks of Google.

You will not find it on the payroll of Amazon or Walmart or General Electric or Samsung.

And as unbelievable as this sounds, there is coming a day when Apple and Google and Amazon and Walmart and General Electric and Samsung will cease to exist.

Only one community and one organization—the community of Christ—will keep existing into eternity.

The way the Bible pictures this community is breathtaking.

There before me was a great multitude that no one could count, from every nation, tribe, people and language, standing before the throne and before the Lamb. They were wearing white robes and were holding palm branches in their hands. And they cried out in a loud voice: "Salvation belongs to our God, who sits on the throne, and to the Lamb."

—Revelation 7:9–10

As you reflect on these words, do you see what John sees? Do you see the wonderful, magnificent, breathtaking picture, a photo mosaic of the bride of Christ? The church?

You simply cannot be a Christian, let alone be a masterpiece, without it.

And this community Jesus planned and formed and unleashed has work to do here.

Chapter 18

ELYSIUM

I love good movies.

And I love good superhero movies.

So, no surprise, my wife and I went to see *Man of Steel*, and as we settled in to watch, one of the previews really caught my attention. In fact, I was so intrigued by it that when we got home, I pulled it up on YouTube, and Erika and I watched it—twice!

I then used it as a premise for an entire sermon.

The preview was of the movie *Elysium*. (It has since been released. I haven't seen it, and I have no desire to watch it.) The preview hit me at many levels.

From watching the preview, I surmised the following:

The premise of the movie is basically this—in a futuristic Earth, this planet of ours is is in ruins. There is destruction everywhere. You can see the poverty, the lack of resources, and the widespread desperation. There is this sense that even God has abandoned Earth. Everything is going downhill.

There is, however, another world—a man-made space station. It is a utopian society, a paradise floating out there somewhere in space. People in that world, called Elysium, live in peace, abundance, privilege, and enjoy optimal health. They are so technologically advanced that if someone gets a disease, say cancer, a machine can eradicate all cancer cells. The people in Elysium look happy. It's the perfect life.

In one world, the people are suffering, but there is total bliss in that other world.

One world is full of pain and poverty, tears and trouble, destruction, death, and despair, but in that other world there is no poverty, no war, no sickness.

I loved the tagline of the movie—it is simply this—*It's better up there!*

The play on the word *Elysium* is quite brilliant, actually.

Elysium was a concept of the afterlife that some Greek philosophers believed in. A place of bliss for the righteous. Homer refers to it in *The Odyssey* (mentioned as Elysian Fields, another name for Elysium):

The Elysian Fields . . .

where life glides on in immortal ease for mortal man;

no snow, no winter onslaught, never a downpour there

but night and day the Ocean River sends up breezes,

singing winds of the West refreshing all mankind.

It's just better up there.

Some interpret that as the primary definition of the gospel.

We will be rescued from this God-forsaken planet, a place full of pain and poverty, tears and trouble, destruction, death, and despair and escape somewhere up there.

That our end goal is to reach for a divine Elysium, somewhere out there in space.

For the rest of eternity, Jesus and us, on Elysium.

A place of peace, abundance, privilege, and enjoying optimal life for all eternity.

A place of total bliss.

A place where there is no more wars, or poverty, or sickness.

Some interpret that to be the gospel—it is better up there!

But is it?

Some of us grew up in traditions that taught us that we need to find Jesus and then one day, we'll escape Earth and find Elysium.

When I attended Eastern University in a small town just outside Philadelphia, Pennsylvania, I learned something different. It opened my eyes in entirely new ways. There was this deep sense on campus that we were not here to simply get Jesus and escape to Elysium, but with Jesus, to bring Elysium to earth.

That God has not forsaken His creation.

He has not given up on His work, His people, His church.

Yes, there is sin, and because of sin there is darkness, and brokenness, and disease, and pain, and death.

And horrible, awful, shocking things happen here on earth.

Little children are sold into slavery.

The weak are exploited.

There's corruption and war and violence.

All this is true and painful and often very difficult to understand.

But the Bible teaches us that the gospel is not just God's rescue plan but also God's redemption and restoration plan.

Paul writes to the church of Colossae:

> For God was pleased to have all his fullness dwell in him, and through him to reconcile to himself all things, whether things on earth or things in heaven, by making peace through his blood, shed on the cross.
> —Colossians 1:19–20

Earlier, Jesus said this:

> I assure you that when the world is made new and the Son of Man sits upon his glorious throne, you who have been my followers will also sit on twelve

thrones, judging the twelve tribes of Israel. And everyone who has given up houses or brothers or sisters or
father or mother or children or property, for my sake,
will receive a hundred times as much in return and will
inherit eternal life. But many who are the greatest now
will be least important then, and those who seem least
important now will be the greatest then.

—Matthew 19:28–30 NLT

When the world is made new! His disciples taught this later on. In
Acts 3:21, Peter says:

For he must remain in heaven until the time
for the final restoration of all things, as God promised
long ago through his holy prophets.

Not that Peter is preaching something new. The redemption and
restoration theme runs throughout the Bible. Long before Peter, the
prophet Isaiah spoke about these things:

See, I will create new heavens and a new
earth. The former things will not be remembered, nor
will they come to mind. —Isaiah 65:17

When His disciples asked Jesus to teach them how to pray, Jesus
taught them to pray:

Our Father in heaven, hallowed be your
name, your kingdom come, your will be done, on
earth as it is in heaven.

—Matthew 6:9–10

New Testament scholar N. T. Wright puts it this way:

> **Jesus' resurrection is the beginning of God's new project not to snatch people away from earth to heaven but to colonize earth with the life of heaven. That, after all, is what the Lord's Prayer is about.**

Because of Jesus, the redemption and restoration process for all creation has begun. It is not fully here yet. As Tim Keller puts it in his book *Center Church*, the "the kingdom of God in the world is *both* 'already' *and* 'not yet.' God is going to restore the creation, but he has not done it yet." Which is why creation anxiously awaits the return of Christ (Romans 8:19–21).

And there is coming a day when everything is going to be set right. When all creation will flourish like God intended it to. When sin will no longer veil and distort the masterpiece we were created to be. When there will be no more hunger, or tears, or pain, or sickness, or death.

Back to N. T. Wright who writes in his book *Simply Christian*:

> **It is a matter of glimpsing that in God's new creation, of which Jesus's resurrection is the start, all that was good in the original creation is reaffirmed. All that has corrupted and defaced it–including many things which are woven so tightly into the fabric of the world as we know it that we can't imagine being without them–will be done away. Learning to live as a Christian is learning to live as a renewed human being, anticipating the eventual new creation in and with a world which is still longing and groaning for that final redemption.**

Genesis tells us about paradise created and lost, Revelation tells us about paradise redeemed and regained. See, if the gospel is not merely a plan to escape from Earth to Elysium, but the grand rescue, redemption, and restoration plan of God, then it has profound implications on how we live our lives in the here and now. It has enormous bearings on the value and worth and purpose of the masterpiece God created us to be—how we live, the choices we make, what we invest our time and talents and resources into. Which means right now, this moment, the Holy Spirit is at work in and through us as part of the unfolding of God's great plan, which He prepared a long time ago.

In the meantime, "we wait for the blessed hope—the appearing of the glory of our great God and Savior, Jesus Christ" (Titus 2:13). And when He does, the kingdom of God will be present in all its glory, there will be a final purge of sin, the obliteration of guilt and shame, the removal of every trace of pain and tears and sorrow.

But we do not wait passively. *We engage with our Lord and Savior, working with Jesus to bring everything back the way it was meant to be.* To bring rescue, renewal, redemption, restoration, and reconciliation to a hurting and needy world.

Dutch theologian Abraham Kuyper put it this way:

There is not a square inch in the whole domain of our human existence over which Christ, who is Sovereign over all, does not cry: "Mine!"

Mine!

Because it is all His!

It was, and will one day be fully His.

And if the gospel is indeed God's grand rescue, redemption, and restoration plan, and if we are indeed masterpieces created by Him and for Him and His purpose, and if Christ is indeed sovereign over the whole domain of human existence, then . . .

It makes sense to rescue children from human trafficking,

It makes sense to bring hope to orphans,

It makes sense to build wells in distant lands
to bring water to the thirsty,

It makes sense to feed the hungry,

It makes sense to clothe the naked,

It makes sense to visit those in prison,

It makes sense to care for the sick,

It makes sense to bring life and soul
into the boardrooms and cubicles,

It makes sense to see raising our children in the way
of the Lord as a mission,

It makes sense to redeem our homes, our workplaces,
our neighborhoods, our cultures,

It makes sense to engage fully
with a mindset that we are not our own, but that
we are jars of clay carrying priceless treasure,

Masterpieces being made to serve the purpose
of the Master Artist.

Then the only meaningful way to live our lives is to allow
Jesus to be our Lord and Savior,

So He can make us who He created us to be,

So that we can engage with Him to do the good works He
has prepared for us to do,

For the redemption and restoration of our world.

We want this.

We need this.

It is our soul's greatest need and desire and longing.

In his book *Secrets in the Dark*, Frederick Buechner calls this our inbuilt sense of being homesick:

> **If we only had eyes to see and ears to hear and wits to understand, we would know that the Kingdom of God in the sense of holiness, goodness, beauty is as close as breathing and is crying out to born both within ourselves and within the world; we would know that the Kingdom of God is what we all of us hunger for above all other things even when we don't know its name or realize that is what we're starving to death for. The Kingdom of God is where our best dreams come from and our truest prayers. We glimpse it at those moments when we find ourselves being better than we are and wiser than we know. We catch sight of it when at some moment of crisis a strength seems to come to us that is greater than our own strength. The Kingdom of God is where we belong. It is home, and whether we realize it or not, I think we are all of us homesick for it.**

The way the story ends is captured by John in Revelation 21:1–5:

> Then I saw "a new heaven and a new earth," for the first heaven and the first earth had passed away, and there was no longer any sea. I saw the Holy City, the new Jerusalem, coming down out of heaven from God, prepared as a bride beautifully dressed for her husband. And I heard a loud voice from the throne saying, "Look! God's dwelling place is now among the people, and he will dwell with them. They will be his people, and God himself will be with them and be

their God. 'He will wipe every tear from their eyes. There will be no more death' or mourning or crying or pain, for the old order of things has passed away." He who was seated on the throne said, "I am making everything new!" Then he said, "Write this down, for these words are trustworthy and true."

Jesus' plan was that we, His followers, will trust Him, follow Him, function under His lordship 24/7/365, and engage fully with Him in the restoration of all things. Because one day, Earth will be our Elysium. In the meantime, we live in the age of disruption.

Chapter 19

DISRUPTION

The phrase *disruptive innovation* was coined by highly esteemed Harvard Business School professor, Clayton Christensen. He writes extensively about this in his books aimed at business executives titled *The Innovator's Dilemma* and *The Innovator's Solution*.

Since then, the concept has gone viral. So what is this thing called disruptive innovation? There are longer definitions and charts and models on this, but for the purpose of this book and to put it simply, disruptive innovation happens when something new comes along that surpasses, displaces, or supplants something old. It could be a new market, a new product, or a new technology that surpasses, displaces, or supplants an old market or product or company.

One example: the Model T and how it surpassed, displaced, and, in one sense, supplanted the horse and carriage industry of its day.

In our age, we have seen this taking place in multiple realms with the advent of the Internet.

Digital cameras surpassing, displacing, and supplanting the traditional film roll cameras and companies. Movie and television streaming services destroying rental shops. Webstores displacing bookstores. Digital downloads surpassing the CD industry. These are just some examples of disruptive innovation in our time.

There are lots of articles and opinions on what was or is the best and greatest disruptive innovation of all time. Some argue it was the personal computer, some say it is Starbucks or the iPhone or Netflix.

So while thinking on this, I remembered a passage in Revelation.

He that sat upon the throne said, Behold, I make all things new. And he said unto me, Write: for these words are true and faithful.

—Revelation 21:5 KJV

So, with all due respect to the business gurus who write about this subject, I believe the best and greatest example of disruptive innovation is not the Model T, it's not Starbucks or personal computers or electricity or the industrial revolution or even the iPhone.

I believe the best and greatest example of disruptive innovation took place 2,000 years ago. For millennia, God watched the sin and the darkness and the oppression and the wreckage and the pain and the injustice, and at first He chose a people to bless and make a blessing. But they disobeyed. And yet, God would not relent in His pursuit of them. He kept disrupting their ways with prophetic voices.

Finally, God decided to send the biggest disruption of all. And He did it by bursting into the scene as a babe in a manger in the person of Jesus. He came down, became one of us, would grow up, and die on the Cross, and rise again so that He can begin a new work in and through us.

It was disruptive in the best sense of the word. This disruption is not some violent overthrow of government or regime change or underground insurgency. Interestingly, that was exactly what some people thought Jesus had come to do. But the disruption Jesus started is a winsome, countercultural, head-scratching, self-sacrificing alternative way of living. It disrupted all the wrong, all the injustice, all the greed, all the hatred and violence and sin—God disrupted all that and put the punishment that brought us upon Jesus. By His wounds we are healed. The frames that bound us were destroyed at the Cross. *On the Cross, the old is being destroyed, it is being surpassed, displaced, and supplanted by something new.*

And this disruption not only took the old frames away, it revealed a new you and a new me, the way we were created to be!

Anyone who belongs to Christ has become a new person. The old life is gone; a new life has begun!
—2 Corinthians 5:17 NLT

Each of you is now a new person. You are becoming more and more like your Creator.
—Colossians 3:10 CEV

But now, by dying to what once bound us, we have been released from the law so that we serve in the new way of the Spirit, and not in the old way of the written code.
—Romans 7:6

This is *God's modus operandi*. He's been doing this from the beginning. He disrupted the chaos with order, darkness with light, bringing forth creation and beauty and splendor. That's His nature.

He comes to a man named Abram and tells him to leave his homeland (Genesis 12). His life has just been disrupted. God comes to Moses through a burning bush and tells him he is to set His people free (Exodus 3). His life has just been disrupted. God sends the angel Gabriel to a poor, young woman named Mary to tell her she has been chosen to give birth to the Messiah (Luke 1). Her life has just been disrupted.

Jesus walks over to Matthew one day. He is a tax collector. Jesus says to him, "Follow me" (Matthew 9:9). Matthew does, and his life has just been disrupted.

God does a disruptive innovation in their lives, and then once they get it, their lives are used to create disruptive innovation in the lives of others. *God is doing a new thing in my life, in your life, on our planet. It is going to be disruptive.*

The goal of this disruption is to first tear down the old frames and paintings in our lives, to reveal the new you and the new me, and then become the masterpiece He created us to be, individually and collectively as the community of Christ and bring disruption in the lives of others.

And so because of Jesus and His work in and through us and in and through His church:

Love is going to disrupt hate.

Joy is going to disrupt pain.

Grace is going to disrupt judgment.

Hope is going to disrupt despair.

Acceptance is going to disrupt isolation and rejection.

Redemption is going to disrupt sin and shame.

And the church that Jesus started,

it continues to flourish in every country

and becomes the lead agent of disruption

when it comes to loneliness, injustice, suffering,

sickness, hatred, and hopelessness.

Christianity is fundamentally disruptive. Disruptive of darkness and injustice and sin and pain and suffering and isolation and hatred and shame.

If you read the Prophets, then into the Gospels, or simply read Mary's song in Luke 1, you will find dozens of examples of the disruptive nature of God's work in and through our lives. Jesus would tell stories that would sound wildly disruptive to His listeners—stories of a banquet where "losers" like the poor, the crippled, the blind, and the lame get invited (Luke 14:15–23), where outsiders like the Samaritans become heroes (10:25–37), where insiders like the Pharisees get told off (11:37–54). Jesus would behave in ways that were wildly disruptive and countercultural. He would mix with people who should have been excluded. He would eat with people no one would eat with. He would become friends with people no one wanted as a friend. He would break rules when it interfered with the flow of God's grace and mercy and love.

If you are in Christ, your life will be disruptive—first to you, then to others.

A few years ago, I was standing in a remote part of India with a team made up of people from various parts of the United States. We were in the middle of one of the poorest districts in the region. There were no brick-and-mortar structures. Mostly huts. We had been invited to join a community of lepers that lived in the wilderness. Having been ostracized by their villages, they were outcasts. If they ventured anywhere near the villages, they had to shout "leper, leper" so people could avoid them.

Our hearts broke for these destitute people, and we committed to help build a residential facility for them. A couple of years after that, we held a medical camp. Several medical professionals from America were there. At the end of the day, we laughed and ate with the lepers. Then, a spontaneous party broke out. Someone had a boom box and played a Bollywood song. Then one leper pulled one of the team members to the middle. Then more people joined in laughing and dancing. Poor, rural, illiterate lepers dancing with affluent, highly educated, and accomplished medical professionals from America. Picture that.

Then one of the medical professionals, who is not a Christian, who had paid his way there and had to take vacation days to go to India, pulled one team member aside and said, "That was the most amazing thing I have ever done in my life. When can we do this again?"

What's going on?

Because of Jesus, a disruptive work of goodness and mercy and love and justice has begun. And when we get a taste of it, when we take part in it, when we see it and feel it and sense it, we start to see the masterpiece we were created to be.

You can take this one story and multiply it a million times across the length and breadth of our world, and you would do it without the least bit of exaggeration. This is the kind of disruption Jesus had in mind when He taught us to pray the Lord's Prayer (Matthew 6:9–13).

Listen to it again:

Our Father in heaven,
hallowed be your name,

> (Aren't we praying for disruption to take place in all the ways we divide and judge each other?
> If we have a common heavenly Father,
> then all are welcome in the family—
> Jews and Gentiles, men and women, slave and free.
> Every person gets to come in.)

your kingdom come,
your will be done,
on earth as it is in heaven.

> (Aren't we praying for disruption to all *other* kingdoms and systems and rivals that resist and battle and compete with the kingdom of God?)

Give us today our daily bread.

> (Aren't we praying for disruption of all the idols of self and pride, knowing that
> all good gifts ultimately come from God?)

And forgive us our debts,
as we also have forgiven our debtors.

> (Aren't we praying for disruption of self-righteousness
> and vengeance and getting even
> in recognition of true grace and love and mercy and jus-
> tice?)

And do not lead us into temptation,
but deliver us from the evil one.
For Yours is the kingdom and the power and the glory forever.
Amen.

> (When you stop to consider the depth of that last line,
> isn't this professing allegiance to Someone
> ahead of anything else in our world?
> Then again, isn't this entire prayer a highly disruptive
> prayer, a battle cry, a cry for things to be as they were
> meant to be?)

Millions of masterpieces, praying this prayer, coming together, and working together disrupting the darkness with light to create the photo mosaic of the image of the kingdom of God coming to earth. That's the real masterpiece. *We* are God's masterpiece. The bride, the body, the community of Christ, the church. And we disrupt darkness, hatred, injustice, and hopelessness.

But we live with this tension of seeing what is and knowing what can be.

Chapter 20

TENSION

*L*et's look at the Lord's Prayer again. It started off when the disciples came to Jesus and saw Him praying. After He finished, one of them spoke up, "Lord, teach us to pray" (Luke 11:1).

Jesus answered, "When you pray, say: 'Our Father in heaven, Hallowed be Your name. Your kingdom come. Your will be done on earth as it is in heaven'" (v. 2).

Because of Jesus, heaven is coming down to earth. His kingdom, His will happening on earth as it is in heaven. Good news!

But then the unthinkable happens.

On April 15, 2013, the Boston Marathon began on a bright and cheery morning without any indication of what was to happen that afternoon. Nearly 25,000 people participated, making their way amid cheers and encouragement from many bystanders. They all headed to Copley Square, 26.2 miles from the starting point.

At exactly 2:49 p.m., two pressure cooker bombs exploded not far from Copley Square. Eight-year-old Martin Richard was the youngest of three people who were killed. The explosions injured 264 others, blowing off limbs, embedding shrapnel, creating a war zone. The area rapidly became a 15-block crime scene.

In the seconds after the blasts, people were in panic. Many dropped their belongings, running to find a safe place. At least one news outlet reported rumors that there might be other bombs. Many of us can recall the aftermath of that incident as

Boston came to a standstill and a massive manhunt began for the killers.

In the aftermath of the Boston bombings, what most people didn't see were the hundreds of stories that started to emerge that did not receive as much coverage, stories that need telling because they show another dynamic at play. It represents the best in America, in us, in our culture, and it paints the picture of something deep within us.

In the minutes after the blasts, as many people were running away from the scene, Army Sgt. Bernard Madore, 1st Lt. Steve Fiola, Staff Sgt. Mark Welch, and 12 other soldiers from the Massachusetts National Guard ran *toward* the scene. They had just finished the marathon in full combat gear, but for the next several hours, they would pull down chain-link fences to allow first responders access to the scene.

Former National Football League player Joe Andruzzi and his wife, Jen, were at the finish line congratulating runners. When he saw the carnage, the 290-pound former lineman ran toward the scene and picked up an injured woman and helped her to an aid tent.

Carlos Arredondo was at the Boston Marathon not as a runner but to honor his son, Marine Lance Cpl. Alexander Scott Arredondo, who died in Iraq in 2004. Carlos was handing out American flags when the blasts went off. Carlos ran toward the scene and saw an injured man. He snuffed the flames off the man's clothing, pinched closed an artery, and rushed him to get medical care, saving his life.

A *Boston Globe* employee hit upon the idea of creating a spreadsheet for Bostonians to offer temporary housing or transportation to victims of the attack. He posted it on the *Boston Globe* website at 5:39 p.m. Within three minutes, more than 100 people had signed up. Within 30 minutes, more than 1,000 Bostonians had opened their homes to strangers affected by the disaster.

Liz Kosearas of Huntington Beach, California, felt compelled to do something to help the victims and first responders. She figured all these people needed to eat. So she took to Reddit and created a page called Random Acts of Pizza. Soon people from all around the United States and the world were donating pizzas. She connected the donations with a local pizza joint in Cambridge, Massachusetts, called Anytime Pizza, who delivered hundreds of pizzas to victims, shelters, hospitals, and fire and police departments. They worked all night and stopped around 5:30 the next morning when all their supplies were gone.

As the first news of the explosions reached the hospitals, doctors and nurses worked around the clock to clear operating rooms and emergency rooms and quickly made plans on how to respond to the crisis. The impact of their actions was that they did not lose a single person of the more than 260 victims that reached these hospitals alive.

NBC Sports posted a tweet, saying, "Reports of marathon runners that crossed finish line and continued to run to Mass General Hospital to give blood to victims." A few hours later, American Red Cross was compelled to respond by saying they had enough blood to meet demand!

As I read about these unsung heroic acts, I thought of Hebrews 13:16 (NLT):

> And don't forget to do good and to share with those in need. These are the sacrifices that please God.

To do good and share with those in need is intricately woven into the second part of Ephesians 2:10. The good works He has planned for us to do is in the here and now, and the world is badly in need of it.

As we scan the news to see what is happening on our planet, we quickly see a kingdom at work. A kingdom of selfishness, arrogance, greed, pride, sin, and violence. Terrorist attacks on different continents, hundreds of little girls kidnapped, corruption in high places, hatred between groups of people, burning of churches, wars and civil wars, more than 3 million children dying each year because of starvation, 132 million orphans, 60 million people displaced from their homes because of conflict and war, 1.1 billion lacking access to safe water, broken nations, broken communities, broken families, broken people.

We look at all of that, and all we can sometimes see is how the kingdom of Earth operates. *We look at the sin and the wreckage and the brokenness and the violence and the victims, and sometimes it's easy to lose heart.* To think that is perhaps the end of the story.

The gospel of Jesus Christ insists it is not. There is indeed another dynamic at play. The Bible teaches that God never abandoned His creation. And He did not abandon us. Repeatedly, throughout Scripture we find God is calling people to a different dynamic, a different reality, a different code of living. There is another kingdom at work.

It doesn't get the news coverage. It may even escape our attention. We can lose heart and like Elijah cry out that no one seems to be following God's way (1 Kings 19:18). We need to be reminded, like Elijah was reminded, there are thousands—and in our case millions—that have not bowed down to Baal.

If you look closely, you will find this thing called the church. It is present in every country, in the most unexpected places, and the dynamic of the kingdom of God is working in the most unpredictable ways. That hope and light and joy and redemption is also at work. That while there are millions of orphans in our world, there are also millions being cared for in the name of Jesus. That while there are a billion people in poverty, there are also millions of microbusinesses and poverty alleviation programs being enacted in the name of Jesus. That while there are disasters and crises and wars, there are also millions being aided in the name of Jesus. That while many in our world would bypass lepers, the homeless, and the destitute, there are also millions of lepers and homeless and destitute people being loved and supported in the name of Jesus.

But we live in the tension, don't we?

The tension of seeing the kingdom of Earth the way it is and the longing (Scripture calls it "groaning," see Romans 8:22) to see the kingdom of God break out in our midst.

I believe this longing is what compels us, whether we know it or not, to move toward the higher calling like many of the people who ran toward the scene in Boston did, whether they realized it or not. It is a holy urge, a sacred impulse, a profound calling deeply embedded in our psyche and our soul.

We long for the day when God will set all things right. In the meantime, God's massive rescue plan is at work. And it is happening right now.

> For he has rescued us from the kingdom of darkness and transferred us into the Kingdom of his dear Son, who purchased our freedom and forgave our sins.
>
> —Colossians 1:13–14

I think the Boston Marathon bombing incident showed us how we can be our best even in the midst of a horrific day. It is also illustrative of the ways God's kingdom dynamic works—bringing hope and life and healing in the midst of despair and death.

In his book, *Simply Good News*, N. T. Wright tells us:

The resurrection declared that Jesus was not the ordinary sort of political king, a rebel leader, that some had supposed. He was the leader of a far larger, more radical revolution than anyone had ever supposed. He was inaugurating a whole

new world, a new creation, a new way of being human. He was forging a way into a new cosmos, a new era, a form of existence hinted at all along but never before unveiled.

And it is here now.

Just think about the millions of churches and orphanages and schools and hospitals and charitable nonprofits and aid organizations that have been founded under the banner of Christ. Think about all the church missions work, all the financial aid, all the projects, all the food drives, all the homeless shelters, all the medical camps, all the soup kitchens, all the rescue missions, all the sponsored kids, and on and on and on. All of it under this premise—that because of Jesus, God's will and His kingdom has now come, and His reign has begun.

Yet, we live in this tension of seeing the coming of the kingdom of God because of what Jesus has done, but we wait anxiously for its fullness to arrive, for tears and pain and death and wars and violence and shootings and bombings and burnings to end. The Bible insists there is a day coming when that will happen—when our groaning and longing and yearning will end, and God Himself will dwell with us in a creation healed and restored to its original state.

The everyday folks who helped out in Boston that day—none of them became very famous or made a fortune—ended up as a footnote to a larger story. There are many others about whom we will never know. They simply responded to an inner impulse to help, to restore, and to bring hope and healing in the middle of suffering.

And there are millions of us, little masterpieces, footnotes in a larger story, and we show up to bring hope and healing in a world desperately in need of it. If the scales were to fall off our eyes, we would see that our world is filled end to end with these little masterpieces, weaving our planet in a fabric of hope and healing and love and moving it toward the fulfillment of the plan of Jesus—His will being done and His kingdom coming on earth as it is in heaven. Yes, we live in this tension, and some days are worse than others, but . . .

Never lose heart.
Never despise the little things you can do and are doing.
Never think you are alone.

Chapter 21

UNKNOWNS

All the way back in Exodus, we learn about a guy named Bezalel. Moses describes him this way in Exodus 35:30–33:

> See, the LORD has chosen Bezalel . . . He has filled him with the Spirit of God, with wisdom, with understanding, with knowledge and with all kinds of skills—to make artistic designs for work in gold, silver and bronze, to cut and set stones, to work in wood and to engage in all kinds of artistic crafts.

Bezalel, along with another guy, Oholiab, oversee the building of the Tabernacle. After the building of the Tabernacle, we don't hear anything more about them.

Even while on the run from his son, Absalom, David and his people were provided food and supplies by Shobi, Makir, and Barzillai (2 Samuel 17:27–28). Although we can read a little more about Barzillai, we do not know anything more about Shobi and Makir.

In 2 Samuel 23, we find a fascinating list of names, some of them with short but intriguing autobiographical notes. These were David's mighty men. We don't know a whole lot more about most of them.

In 2 Kings 5:2–3, we find the captivating little story about a young girl, taken as a slave from her homeland and serving in the household of Naaman. She is a slave and remains nameless in the story, yet she points Naaman through his wife to the true and living God. We don't know anything more about her.

In Judges 7, we find the remarkable story of Gideon and his army of 300 men who go on to win a decisive victory against overwhelming odds. Who were these 300 men? There is no record or history or monument to these men.

At the end of the Book of Romans (see chapter 16), Paul talks about these people:

Phoebe

Priscilla and Aquila

Mary

Andronicus and Junia

Ampliatus

Urbanus

Apelles

Aristobulus

Herodion

Narcissus

Tryphena and Tryphosa

Persis

Rufus

Asyncritus, Phlegon, Hermes, Patrobas, Hermas, and the other brothers and sisters with them.

Philologus, Julia, Nereus and his sister, and Olympas

Who are these people? What do we know about them?

At the end of his letter to the church at Colossae (see Colossians 4:7–15), Paul mentions a bunch of names with fascinating hints:

Tychicus, a dear brother, a faithful minister and fellow servant in the Lord

Onesimus, faithful and dear brother

Aristarchus, a fellow prisoner

Mark, the cousin of Barnabas

Jesus, who is called Justus

*Epaphras, a servant of Christ Jesus, always wrestling
    in prayer*

Luke, the beloved doctor

Demas

Nympha, who hosted a house church in her home

How much more do we really know about most of these people?

Paul is in Athens. He brings the good news to the people there in a brilliant, remarkably anointed, and culturally contextualized sermon. Then, Luke writes in Acts 17:34:

Some of the people became followers of Paul and believed. Among them was Dionysius, a member of the Areopagus, also a woman named Damaris, and a number of others.

Dionysius was a member of the Areopagus, likely a judge. We don't know who Damaris was or the others. There is no mention of this little church of Athens again in the Book of Acts. There is no record of Paul ever having gone back there. A prominent citizen of Athens and a few others became Christian. They formed a tiny fellowship of believers in a city full of idols. Then what happened? We simply do not know.

A couple chapters later, Paul arrives at Ephesus. Then the text tells us in Acts 19:10:

⌇This went on for two years, so that all the Jews and Greeks who lived in the province of Asia heard the word of the Lord.

Who exactly were these people? What were their names? We do not know.

So, again, who are all these people? What do we know about them? Not very much, except that they were from all sorts of different cultural, social, economic backgrounds. The list included men and women, Jews and Gentiles, wealthy and well-known people at the time, and free men and women and prisoners.

The fact is, as far as we know, they didn't gain a whole lot of fame and fortune by following Jesus. Most didn't receive applause, adoration, or approval from the public. There were no monuments or shrines or plaques erected in their honor. They served quietly, tirelessly, and faithfully. In fact, many ended up in chains, as prisoners, and were beaten, crucified, tortured, and thrown to the lions.

Hebrews 11 is known as The Great Hall of Faith or the Faith Hall of Fame. The chapter starts by recounting the faith of Abel and then goes on to name some of the greatest heroes of faith in the Bible—Enoch, Noah, Abraham, Sarah, Isaac, Jacob, Joseph, Moses, Rahab, Gideon, Samson, David, Samuel, and so on.

And then, at the end of Hebrews 11, the writer makes a poignant reminder of the kinds of things some people faced because of Jesus.

⌇Others were made fun of and beaten with whips, and some were chained in jail. Still others were stoned to death or sawed in two or killed with swords. Some had nothing but sheep skins or goat skins to wear. They were poor, mistreated, and tortured. The world did not deserve these good people, who had to wander in deserts and on mountains and had to live in caves and holes in the ground.

—Hebrews 11:36–38 CEV

But the big differentiator was this: "All of them pleased God because of their faith!" (v. 39 CEV).

We may not know a whole lot about them, but they are all known by God. They are precious in His sight. All of them!

This is what it means to live for an audience of One.

Let's go back to that big photo mosaic. It is possible that as you serve the Lord, your photo may not be seen by many, it may not be recognized by many, it may not even be counted as significant by many.

And then the writer of Hebrews makes a beautiful exhortation:

Therefore, since we are surrounded by such a great cloud of witnesses, let us throw off everything that hinders and the sin that so easily entangles. And let us run with perseverance the race marked out for us, fixing our eyes on Jesus, the pioneer and perfecter of faith. For the joy set before him he endured the cross, scorning its shame, and sat down at the right hand of the throne of God. Consider him who endured such opposition from sinners, so that you will not grow weary and lose heart.

—Hebrews 12:1–3

As you serve the Lord, and as you strive to be the masterpiece He created you to be, and as you find your place in the great photo mosaic of the church, maybe your work and your life and your story will be noticed and celebrated. Maybe that might never happen.

That's not the point though.

It's about the heart.

Are you willing to be like the many unmentioned,
unsung, unnamed heroes of the Bible?

Are you willing to be an unknown for Christ?

To forgo the need for the applause,
the adoration, the approval.

To know that there may not be any monuments and shrines
and plaques erected in your honor.

To continue to serve quietly, tirelessly, and faithfully.

To know without any doubt that you are indeed
living for an audience of One.

To know that your name may not end up in the first half
of Hebrews 11 on this side of eternity.

It may end up in the last section among "others."

But that you will be counted among those
about whom it has been said,

"All of them pleased God because of their faith!"

To know that there is Someone to whom
your individual photo and masterpiece is important
and precious and beloved—and that it fulfills a critical role
in the big picture.

And then there will come a day when you will look into the loving, appreciative, delighted face of your Master as He looks deep into your eyes and says:

Well done, good and faithful servant! You have been faithful with a few things; I will put you in charge of many things. Come and share your master's happiness!
—Matthew 25:21

EPILOGUE

I pray that out of his glorious riches

he may strengthen you with power through his Spirit

in your inner being,

so that Christ may dwell in your hearts through faith.

And I pray that you, being rooted and established in love,

may have power, together with all the Lord's holy people,

to grasp how wide

and long

and high

and deep

is the love of Christ,

and to know this love that surpasses knowledge—

that you may be filled to the measure of all the fullness of God.

Now to him who is able to do

immeasurably more than all we ask or imagine,

according to His power that is at work within us,

to him be glory in the church and in Christ Jesus

throughout all generations,

for ever and ever!

Amen.

—Ephesians 3:16–21

STUDY GUIDE

YOU (REMIXED)

Read Psalm 139 in two or three different versions.

Which parts of this chapter do you find easy to believe as they pertain to you? Which parts are difficult to believe? Why?

What does "fearfully and wonderfully made" mean to you?

How does the author's point that God thinks of you a lot strike you in your current situation?

Part One
THE HIDDEN MASTERPIECE

CHAPTER 1
HIDDEN

Do you often spend time critiquing yourself, thinking about labels and remarks other people make about you? What does that do to you and your sense of identity?

Moses, Solomon, Jeremiah, and others felt inadequate to the task God called them to. Is God calling you to be someone who does something, and is your response to that similar to theirs?

Do you believe God created you to be a masterpiece? If yes, is the masterpiece shining and visible, or is it shrouded and hidden? If no, what makes you think that?

CHAPTER 2
FLEA MARKET

Do you agree with the author that the masterpiece God created you to be is often hidden under other versions of you?

Is there a "Ford" you are currently driving you need to get rid of?

The author makes the point that when we stop expecting God to do anything of great kingdom impact through our lives, we start to pray little prayers and exercise little faith. Do you agree?

Do you sometimes get a gnawing sense that bubbles up through life's distractions, demands, and difficulties that there's got to be something more to your life than its current state?

Part Two
FRAME

CHAPTER 3
EVERYTHING/NOTHING

Read 2 Corinthians 6:1–10. What is the overriding emotion you sense from Paul?

As you read the author's argument juxtaposing the achievements of America and its state of mind, where do you see your community and your life in this?

The author maintains that it is possible to live a life of "old paintings and frames" and come to a realization that you don't possess it, but it possesses you. Has this ever happened in your life? To others close to you?

Have you ever paused long enough to listen to your soul's cry?

CHAPTER 4
LONGING

Read the story of the rich young ruler in Mark 10:17–31 (and for good measure, read it also in Luke 18:18–30). What are some words you would use to describe the life of this young man?

Do you think stuff or the quest for stuff can squelch the cry of our souls? So then, where is the balance?

The author makes the point that part of the reason why we rush so much is that we are constantly reaching for something just outside our grasp. Do you agree?

A soul that seeks after God but says no to God, will always be disheartened. Why would anyone say no to God? Why is our soul not at rest when we say no to God?

For the rich young man, his great possessions trumped the Lordship of Jesus in his life. What are some other things that can trump the Lordship of Christ in our lives?

CHAPTER 5
PAST—1

Read John 4:1–42. What were some of the old paintings and frames that shrouded and masked the real masterpiece for the Samaritan woman?

The author lists four ways we try to deal with sin on our own—try harder, fake it, become legalistic, or simply get discouraged. Do you think this is fairly common among followers of Jesus today? Is there a way you most typically try to deal with sin on your own?

If you struggle with past sin and choices, read 2 Corinthians 5:17; Isaiah 65:16; Colossians 1:13–14; and Philippians 3:13–14. What is Scripture telling you about how to deal with your past?

CHAPTER 6
PAST—2

What are your worst fears?

What or who shaped your image or identity of who you are early on in life?

How does the author's argument on how people deal with shame match with your life experiences?

Read Mark 5:21–43; Matthew 9:18–26; and Luke 8:40–56. Track the woman's story of one long journey from the old paintings and frames to a transformed identity.

CHAPTER 7
SPARK

The author defines a soul spark as that defining moment when the human soul rises above the everyday and catches a glimpse of what a true masterpiece could be. Have you ever experienced the spark the author is talking about?

Favio looked at what was around him and became a channel for blessing. What is around you? Where can you be a blessing?

What stirs you to your core?

Part Three
PICTURE

CHAPTER 8
BIRTH

Have you ever looked at your birth certificate? What does a birth certificate tell us about a person? What are some questions you wish were answered when you were born?

Read Genesis 2:7; Isaiah 43:7; Colossians 1:16; and Proverbs 16:4 again. What do they tell you about you?

Do you agree with the author that the very first step to understanding who we were meant to be is to start by understanding who our Creator is?

CHAPTER 9
GOD

Looking over the four views of God (authoritarian, benevolent, critical, or distant), which one do you think people in our culture and in our time have most come to identify with? Why is that? Which do you identify with most?

How does the statement by Paul Froese strike you—"A person's conception of God is central to how they perceive their world and behave in it"?

Read John 1:1–14, and allow the enormity of this passage to sink in. Now reread chapter 9. Are there any other insights you have gained in what the writer is telling us in John 1?

When you read the author's scriptural description of who Jesus is and how Jesus views you, what does that mean in terms of your life's purpose this day, this week, and this year?

CHAPTER 10
DEATH TO LIFE

Do a search for Virginia Woolf's essay "Death of a Moth" online and read it. Then read John 5:24; Romans 6:23; and 1 Corinthians 15:54–57. How does our fear or preoccupation with death compare with the promise of Jesus as revealed in Scripture?

What are some ways we live in the tension of life-givers or life-takers?

How does the phrase death to life apply to you in your daily walk with Jesus?

CHAPTER 11
NEW

Read 2 Corinthians 5:17–21. How does the new differ from the old in your life?

What are some of the pros and cons of living in an ascribed status culture? What are some of the pros and cons of living in an achieved status culture?

The author makes the argument that creating a masterpiece takes time. Sometimes all you can see are incremental improvements. Then there are times when it seems like life is one step forward and two steps back. Where are you in your journey to allowing our Savior to make you into His masterpiece?

CHAPTER 12
TALENTS

What do you think of the author's statement that we are all uniformly loved but uniquely gifted?

Do you think there are people who feel like their talents and gifts do not matter? That they are too small, too little, or too insignificant? What would the Master of the Talents say to someone who thinks like that?

The author lists several ways Jesus resources us to build His kingdom—these include everything from words and actions to material resources. What are some ways you are investing into the kingdom of God?

CHAPTER 13
ONE CUP

What is the opportunity of the one cup for you?

Pray that God will remove the scales from your eyes this week. Then write down all the *little* ways God uses you this week.

What do you think of the author's point that when we learn to handle the holiness and the significance and the responsibility of the opportunity of the one cup, we can graduate to the ministry of the two cups?

CHAPTER 14
SILENCE

The author claims there is a furious urgency for calm in our souls. Do you agree?

Have you ever experienced complete silence for more than 30 minutes? What was it like?

The author writes that silence is fasting from noise. How can fasting from noise help us become the masterpiece God created us to be?

Try the experiment the author suggests as a first step if this is new for you—find a quiet space in your life for about 30 minutes and slowly read Psalms 138 and 139, and reflect on them without any distractions.

CHAPTER 15
REMAINS

Are you among those who are going through a very tough time, and you find it hard to believe that God can still use you? How did this chapter speak into your life right now?

Read Isaiah 40:27–31. In what ways can a person wait upon the Lord and gain the kind of strength only He can give?

If all you can see are the pain and the remains of your life, how does the story of Gideon apply to you?

CHAPTER 16
TODAY

Think about yesterday. How did it go? Did you live it in recognition of God's presence?

How can you adopt a Brother Lawrence mindset in your daily life?

In what ways can you give God the glory of being an "awesome Dad" today? How can you repeat this each day?

Part Four
GALLERY

CHAPTER 17
MOSAIC

How did the fact strike you that every pronoun in Ephesians 2 is in the plural? Do you see yourself as a piece of the grand masterpiece of the church that our Lord is building and unleashing to do the good works He has prepared for us to do?

The works are to be good and they are prepared for us to do—what do you think are the works, good and prepared, that God has for you and your community?

The author says you really can't be a masterpiece without being part of the church. Do you agree? Why or why not?

CHAPTER 18
ELYSIUM

What is your view of the gospel—is it the good news that we will one day escape Earth for our ultimate Elysium or is it the good news that heaven has come down?

What do you think of the author's point that the gospel is not just God's rescue plan but also God's redemption and restoration plan?

How does our view of the gospel impact the way we see the role of the masterpiece God has created us to be?

CHAPTER 19
DISRUPTION

What do you think about the author's statement that Christianity is fundamentally disruptive?

Have you ever considered yourself to be disruptive of all the wrong, the injustice, the darkness, and the hopelessness around you?

How does that attitude, in tandem with the ministry of the local church, accomplish the goal of God as laid out in the Lord's Prayer?

CHAPTER 20
TENSION

When you look at world news, do you ever feel overwhelmed and lose hope?

Why do you think the many little stories of hope and healing never register in our minds?

How should we live with joy and hope in the middle of the tension of seeing the kingdom of Earth the way it is and longing for the fullness of the kingdom of God to come?

CHAPTER 21
UNKNOWNS

In a fame- and image-saturated culture like ours, this closing chapter can be hard for a lot of us. Are you willing to be an "unknown" for Jesus? Unknown, that is, to this world but very much known to your Master.

How does the author's point of how so many of God's little masterpieces may not get the recognition in this world strike you?

How will that compare with the words of the Master in the closing paragraph of the book?

ADDITIONAL RESOURCES

We have created great resources to go as a companion to this book. You can download these for free on our website at TheHiddenMasterpiece.com.

You can download the Study Guide in pdf format to use in your small group or book club. You can also download a four-week church campaign kit for free with sermon outlines and suggested plan for your worship service.

Behind the Real Wonders of the World
... Lies a Journey for the Heart

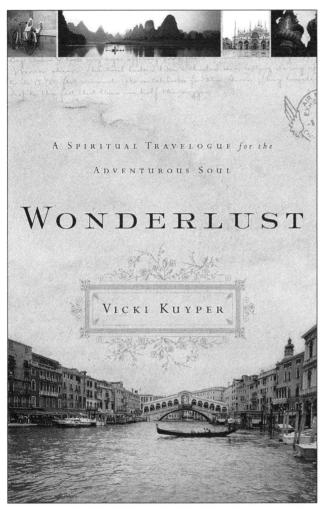

New Hope® Publishers is a division of WMU®, an international organization that challenges Christian believers to understand and be radically involved in God's mission. For more information about WMU, go to wmu.com. More information about New Hope books may be found at NewHopePublishers.com. New Hope books may be purchased at your local bookstore.

Please go to NewHopePublishers.com for more helpful information about *Unearthed*.

If you've been blessed by this book, we would like to hear your story. The publisher and author welcome your comments and suggestions at: newhopereader@wmu.org.